The Relationship Between Second Generation Leaders' Sense of Valuation by First Generation Leaders and Their Retention in the Vietnamese Church in America

RAISING NEXT GENERATION LEADERS

NHIEM THAI TRAN

Copyright © 2015 by Nhiem Thai Tran

THE RELATIONSHIP BETWEEN SECOND GENERATION LEADERS' SENSE OF VALUATION BY FIRST GENERATION LEADERS AND THEIR RETENTION IN THE VIETNAMESE CHURCH IN AMERICA
Raising Next Generation Leaders
by Nhiem Thai Tran

Printed in the United States of America.

ISBN 9781498450201

All rights reserved solely by the author. The author guarantees all contents are original and do not infringe upon the legal rights of any other person or work. No part of this book may be reproduced in any form without the permission of the author. The views expressed in this book are not necessarily those of the publisher.

Unless otherwise indicated, Scripture quotations are taken from the New International Version (NIV). Copyright © 1973, 1978, 1984, 2011 by Biblica, Inc.™. Used by permission. All rights reserved.

www.xulonpress.com

This Dissertation was prepared and presented to the Faculty as a part of the requirements for the Doctoral degree of Ministry at Alliance Theological Seminary, Nyack, New York. All rights and privileges normally reserved by the author as copyright holder are waived for the Seminary. The Seminary Library may catalog, display, and use this Thesis in all normal ways such materials are used, for reference and for other purposes, including electronic and other means of preservation and circulation, including on-line computer access and other means by which library materials are or in the future may be made available to researchers and library users.

TABLE OF CONTENTS

Acknowledgments . . . . **IX**

Abstract XI

CHAPTER 1 13
   Ministry Context: Background of Vietnamese Churches
      Under the Christian and Missionary Alliance 13
   Cultural Context 18
   Vietnamese Pastor As Emperor: A Mentality in Vietnamese
      Churches Today 26
   Culutral Gap Between the First (Older) Generation
      and Second (Younger) Generation Vietnamese in the
      Vietnamese Church in America 33
   Statement of the Ministry Problem 47
   theological Foundations theoretical Approaches
      To Retention and Leadership Development of the Younger
      Generation. 52
   Servant Leadership Style Defined in Scripture 58
   Assumptions 63
   the Model and Purpose of the Research 64
   Hypothesis. 66

CHAPTER 2 . . . .**68**
   Literature Review 68
   Work That Addresses Healthy Vietnamese-American Church Life
      and the Retention of the Vietnamese Younger Generation . .72
   Works That Address Healthy Church Life for
      Korean-American and Other Asian-American Churches . . .73

Works That Address American Church Life and the
Retention of the Younger Generation 84

CHAPTER 3 . . . . **.89**
Methodology 89
Participants 90
Data Collection 93
Data Collection instrument 94

CHAPTER 4 . . . . **.97**
Findings. 97
Survey Results 98

CHAPTER 5 . . . . **.117**
Conclusions. 117
Reflections on the Implications of the Survey Data 124
Church Recommendations 134
Concluding Reflections 141

APPENDICES . . . . **.149**

A SGVFG Scale Survey Questions 149
B Request Letter Sent to Three Groups (A,B,C) 153
C List of Attending Churches of Many Different
Denominations 155
D 157
E 159

WORKS CITED . . . . **.161**

vi

ILLUSTRATIONS AND CHARTS

ILLUSTRATION

Figure 1: Different Perception between East and West 25
Figure 2: Religious Affiliation of Asian-American Population ...46
Table 1: Survey Participants: Group A.................. 155
Table 2: Survey Participants: Group B 157
Table 3: Survey Participants: Group C 159

CHARTS

Chart #1.. 100
Chart#2 103
Chart #3.. 106
Chart #4.. 108
Chart #5.. 111
Chart #6.. 114
Chart #7.. 116

ACKNOWLEDGMENTS

A number of people have supported and motivated me to accomplish this research project of how to engage the younger Vietnamese generations into church leadership and train them to become God's disciples within the immigrant Vietnamese community in America. I wish to acknowledge and honor them here. First, I am greatly indebted to my wife, Ha Thi Hong Nhung, and our four children (Nhat Tran, Nhan Tran, Sion Tran, and Ivy Tran), who have provided a relentless spring of inspiration and support. Second, I am grateful to my father, who was in the communist's re-education camp between 1978-1980 and 1984-1986, for graciously teaching me how to preach and to serve others. Third, I wish to recognize my major professors who have walked me through this pastoral journey: Dr. Frank Chan, who guided me through this dissertation; Dr. Ronald Walborn, who walked me through spiritual journey; and Dr. Martin Sanders, who challenged me with bigger visions and dreams during my study at Alliance Theological Seminary, Nyack, New York, and provided me with much valuable advice and generated in me an interest in Christian

leadership in the global context.

ABSTRACT

The purpose of this study is to analyze the sense of valuation that members of the younger Vietnamese generation receive from church leadership and the effect of this perception of valuation on the church's retention of the younger generation. The motivation for this study arose out of an intergenerational conflict which has existed for some years between the first and second generations of Vietnamese church leaders and members. The researcher proposed that merging potential leaders of the younger Vietnamese generation into church leadership would increase retention of the younger generation in the Vietnamese churches. In order to test this hypothesis, a survey was created and filled out by three groups of second generation Vietnamese: Group A consisted of those who have remained in the Vietnamese Church; Group B included those who had once attended a Vietnamese Church, but have left and are now attending a non-Vietnamese Church; and Group C was comprised of those who once attended a Vietnamese Church, but now are not attending any church. Thus, the participant groups included one "retained" group and two "un-retained" groups. The seven-question survey was designed to evaluate seven possible issues related to retention, each touching in some way upon the Second Generation's sense of valuation by the First Generation. The researcher tabulated and analyzed the differences in the responses between the three groups. The results of the study show that valuation of the younger Vietnamese by the first generation is an essential component for making disciples and retaining and developing future leaders within the immigrant Vietnamese church community.

CHAPTER 1

This chapter will describe the cultural and ministry context of the Vietnamese immigrant churches in America today, including a description of the intergenerational gap between the first and second generation immigrants. This representation of the church will be followed by a summary of the ministry problem as it relates to this study. The theological and theoretical foundations of leadership development within the church will then be examined, and the chapter will conclude with a description of the model and purpose of the research project.

MINISTRY CONTEXT: BACKGROUND OF VIETNAMESE CHURCHES UNDER THE CHRISTIAN AND MISSIONARY ALLIANCE

The story of the Vietnamese Christian and Missionary Alliance Church (C&MA) in America begins with the story of the Vietnamese immigration in the 1970s. After the fall of South Vietnam, when the last United States military troops left Vietnam on March 29, 1973, the communists and the South Vietnamese were already experiencing a postwar war.[1] Two years later, during the last days of April 1975, even though the United States was still providing some military aid to the south, many Vietnamese people, including ordained pastors, escaped the south of Vietnam for freedom before the south was actually overtaken by the communists. Large numbers of these refugees reached American ships off the coast, and many neighboring countries such as Thailand, Hong Kong, and Malaysia established refugee camps for Vietnamese people. This situation prompted an International Rescue Committee in the United States to decide to set up a rescue and resettlement program to work on behalf of Vietnamese refugees. The operations soon brought many Vietnamese refugees from Indochina to California, Arkansas, Florida, and Pennsylvania.[2] In August 1980, another influx of Vietnamese boat people arrived throughout the Southeast Asian countries of Singapore, Thailand, Hong Kong, Korea, Cambodia, Malaysia, and the Philippines.[3]

---

[1] Ronald H. Spector, "Vietnam War" *Encyclopedia Britannica*, Cited 9 April 2014. Online: http://www.britannica.com/EBchecked/topic/628478/Vietnam-War/234639/The-fall-of-South-Vietnam.

[2] George Rupp, "1975: The Largest Refugee Resettlement Effort in American History [IRC at 75]," *International Rescue Committee* (June 27th, 2008), n.p. Cited 9 April 2014. Online: http://www.rescue.org/blog/1975-largest-refugee-resettlement-effort-american-history-irc-75.

[3] Paul Rutledge, *The Role of Religion in Ethnic Self-Identity: A Vietnamese Community* (Lanham, MD: University Press of America, 1985), 1.

Many Vietnamese refugees resettled in America and have chosen the United States as their second home. In the *Role of Religion in Ethnic Self-Identity*, Rutledge exhibits that Vietnamese refugees arrived and scattered to almost every state, wherever there was a sponsorship for their first time relocation in the United States.[4] In fact, Vietnamese immigrants were encouraged to scatter across the 50 states, an intentional effort of a United States' policy which sought to avoid a heavy economic impact on any one state or region. Despite this effort, a high percentage of the Vietnamese refugees eventually chose California as their final destination.[5] However, the immigration process required a cultural shift from the home culture into an enormously different shared environment which demanded a processing period for adaptation.

As America became a new home for many Vietnamese refugees, Vietnamese Christians and pastors saw the need for a weekly gathering to worship God, and they experienced their first time of worshiping the Lord together in America in their first Sunday service on May 4, 1975.[6] Within three months, a total of five Vietnamese churches had been established in Lincoln, San Diego, Orlando, Hawthorne, and North Hollywood, and all of the Vietnamese pastors and Christians

---

[4] Paul Rutledge, 5..

[5] Roy D'Andrade, A Study of Personal and Cultural Values: American, Japanese, and Vietnamese (New York, NY: Palgrave Macmillan, 2008), 78.

[6] Quang Ba Nguyen, *Hội Thánh Ta* (Hội Thánh Tin Lành Việt Nam – Giáo Hạt Việt Nam Hoa Kỳ). (Fullerton, California: 2000), 5.

gathered together for their first conference held at Alliance Theological Seminary in New York on August 4, 1975.[7] After the conference, another 15 Vietnamese churches were established in other states, and there was a total of 23 Vietnamese churches established from 1975 to 1979.[8] Even though Vietnamese churches were new in America and the number of the Vietnamese pastors was limited, between 1979 and 1988, at least 7 additional churches opened to meet the spiritual needs of the many Vietnamese Christians nationwide.[9]

After the first wave of refugees left Vietnam in 1975, many boat people continued to find ways to immigrate as early as 1979, and the number of Vietnamese churches in the United States soared from 30 churches to nearly 60 churches between 1989 and 1997. Many of these Vietnamese boat people had already accepted Christ through evangelists who had come to refugee camps to witness for Christ.[10] Vietnamese-established churches nationwide were able to host these Vietnamese refugee newcomers, which resulted in the existing churches becoming larger in numbers and assuming more responsibilities, like providing accommodations and many other miscellaneous needs, to help these

---

[7] Quang Ba Nguyen, 5.

[8] Ibid., 5-6.

[9] Ibid., 6.

[10] Nghia Minh Vo, *The Vietnamese Boat People, 1954 and 1975–1992* (Jefferson, North Carolina: McFarland & Company, Inc., Publishers, 2006), 152-162.

newcomers resettle in America. Church members were able to help these newcomers learn English, learn to drive, and find jobs.

The last influx of incoming Vietnamese immigrants, between 1990 and 2003, consisted of Vietnamese soldiers and officers who had been associated with the United States Army or had served under the government of South Vietnam. These latest immigrants were those who had been detained in communist re-education camps for 4 to 12 years after the fall of South Vietnam and began to arrive in America later, after they were released.[11] Many of these former officers and former solders of the South Vietnamese government became Christians after they received assistance from the Vietnamese immigrant churches in the United States. However, a majority of these Vietnamese veterans stopped attending church once they were able to take care of themselves or began to receive direct support from their relatives who had resettled prior to their arrival.

The Vietnamese churches in America were established because Vietnamese pastors who had left Vietnam right after the fall of South Vietnam decided that they should continue to serve the Lord in this new land among the Vietnamese immigrants in the United States. Since English was a second language which a majority of the

---

[11] Seth Mydans, "Old Soldiers: The Last Refugees Free to Leave Vietnam," *The New York Times*. Cited 16 December 2014. Online: http://www.nytimes.com/1992/09/14/us/old-soldiers-the-last-refugees-free-to-leave-vietnam.html?src=pm&pagewanted=2&pagewanted=all.

Vietnamese immigrants could not speak fluently, they were encouraged to take English as a second language classes. However, many of the Vietnamese immigrants were not able to continue their education in America, except for those children who had accompanied their parents to America at an early age.

Many of the Vietnamese pastors were among those who did not have the opportunity to pursue further education. These pastors volunteered to plant new Vietnamese immigrant churches in America and made an effort to plant as many new churches as possible within the Vietnamese Christian community during the early 1990s. While the Vietnamese pastors were planting new churches, they often obtained extra work to supplement their family's income, and they did not focus on further academic training in seminaries to equip themselves for their ministries in America.

CULTURAL CONTEXT

Since China has had a very special relationship with Vietnam since the Bronze Age, when the kingdoms of Van Lang (c.800–258 BC) and Au Lac (257–208 BC) in North Vietnam were invaded by the Chinese emperor Wu of the Han Dynasty in 111 BC,[12] Vietnamese culture and

---

[12] Mary Somers Heidhues, *Southeast Asia: A Concise History* (London: Thames & Hudson, 2000), 89.

literature were influenced by the worldview of Confucian orthodoxy due to the dominance of the Chinese empire over Vietnam for over one thousand years. Thus, the Chinese religious worldview was disseminated widely in the Vietnamese territory for centuries.

According to Shelton Woods, the Chinese empire shaped the Vietnamese world through political, military, and economic power. Furthermore, Woods suggests that historians estimate that the majority of people in Southeast Asia have been influenced by the doctrines of the Chinese scholar, Master Kong Fuzi, known as Confucius (551–479 BC).[13] Confucianism teaches that there are three elements in our universe: heavens, earth, and humanity. In view of this triad, human beings should maintain harmony in the relationships within their families as peacefully as the harmony between the heavens and the earth. Confucius believed that such relationship orders as ruler-subject, father-son, husband-wife, older brother-younger brother, and friend-friend are orders that have been established through the cosmos.

Because of this influence, Confucius greatly impacted the Vietnamese religious system which embraces the virtue of harmony, and it became the goal for households to demonstrate a harmonious way of living between the members within a household. In other words, harmony can be achieved when all members honor the high

---

[13] Shelton Woods, *Vietnam: An Illustrated History* (New York: Hippocrene Books, 2002), 15.

power distance relationships between parents and children, husbands and wives, brothers and sisters, and so on.[14] As a result, Vietnamese immigrants are still heavily influenced by this worldview within the Vietnamese church setting, where the pastor, in the role of overseer, is considered to have the highest power, and others must perform their roles properly according to the hierarchic structure as a principle method of "face-saving" behavior.[15]

In *Cultures and Organizations*, the authors Geert Hofstede, Gert Jan Hofstede, and Michael Minkov convince their readers that trends of power distance are rooted in the family, with varying intensity in different cultures. According to the authors' illustration of the power distance index values for 76 countries and regions, Asian countries, especially Vietnam, are considered to be at the higher end of the power distance scale.[16] Since Vietnam is identified as one of the highest power distance countries in the world, this characteristic is evident in its high power distance relationships; children are subject to show their obedience toward their parents, and a younger brother or sister should also submit to the older siblings within a household.[17] Power and authority

---

[14] Paul Rutledge, *The Role of Religion in Ethnic Self-Identity: A Vietnamese Community* (Lanham, New York: University Press of America, 1985), 29.

[15] Ibid., 29.

[16] Geert Hofstede, Gert Jan Hofstede, and Michael Minkov, *Cultures and Organizations: Intercultural Cooperation and Its Importance for Survival* (New York: McGraw Hill, 2010), 58-59.

[17] Ibid., 67.

issues are of prime importance, and every member of the household must practice them every day; this is a basic virtue according to the worldview of Confucianism. Without a doubt, this tradition has influenced the Vietnamese churches worldwide.

Therefore, according to the present author's evaluation, if the reader looks at a church as a workplace, there is no doubt that the first-generation Vietnamese who resettled in the United States are still practicing their cultural power distance relationship patterns within the church, wherein the pastor is the supreme power and others are subordinate, lacking authority and equality. This relationship persists because such traditions have been ingrained in the minds of a country in which Confucianism has dominated for centuries. As a result, the title of pastor within the Vietnamese church tradition has been enhanced to a symbolically dominant title to make him look as powerful as possible.[18]

In Chinese society, people believe that the emperor who dwells on the throne is given the power to rule by deities from heaven, and thus, showing submission to an emperor is an act of obedience, similar to a person submitting him or herself to deities in heaven. In other words, an earthly emperor is a mediator between the heavens and earth, and subjects should be eager to please their emperor.[19] Because the

---

[18] Geert Hofstede, Gert Jan Hofstede, and Michael Minkov, 77.

[19] Shelton Woods, *Vietnam: An Illustrated History* (New York: Hippocrene Books, 2002), 18.

Chinese religious doctrine has been influencing Vietnamese lives for more than one thousand years, this mindset has become entrenched in the Vietnamese consciousness from generation to generation. As a matter of fact, today, many of the Vietnamese church leaders worldwide still view the pastoral role with the perception that this position is beyond attainment for most people—a position full of power and splendor.[20] Recognizing the benefits of this position, many Vietnamese Christians passionately seek to become a pastor in order to obtain such glory with a title to impress others, and pursuing this title becomes an idol for many first-generation Vietnamese, both in Vietnam and outside of Vietnam. These culturally high power distance traditions have been built from generation to generation, and Vietnamese people do not have any doubts about the power of their leaders or their responsibility to show submission.

Furthermore, when the communist regime began to take control in the south, the communist government continued to use force to control all civilians who had served under the former government.[21] They took the lives of many of these government servants and put others in re-education camps after the fall of the South; in addition, they tor-

---

[20] Paul Rutledge, *The Role of Religion in Ethnic Self-Identity: A Vietnamese Community* (Lanham, MD: University Press of America, 1985), 29.

[21] Michael Benge, "Vietnam: How the Communist Grinches Stole Christmas," n.p. Cited 13 March 2015. Online: http://www.frontpagemag.com/2015/michael-benge/vietnam-how-the-communist-grinches-stole-christmas/.

tured family members, such as soldiers' spouses and children who remained at home. Police stations nationwide used loudspeakers to announce their propaganda regularly from early morning till late evening, Monday to Sunday, with a very loud voice through a cassette tape that recorded the lecturer in advance to make sure the entire block of each precinct heard about the war victories of the communists.

Besides brainwashing people in the re-education camps and through the loudspeaker recordings, the communists also ordered every teenager from each household to wake up early every morning for a name check at the local police station; this was known as a mobilization order and occurred from 1978 to 1986. The local communist police station did this to make sure that people would know who was in control of the country. At the same time, a police official could give an order for any person to come to their nearby station to be interrogated if there was anything that looked suspicious. Many first-generation pastors replicate these practices within their church groups, as they believe that they have authority to interrupt a group's discussion or meeting at any time.

Because of the use of such propaganda to abuse people's freedom of speech, Vietnamese civilians experienced many years of suffering under the communist government, but they also became accustomed to the communist propaganda. Ironically, as mentioned above, the first-generation Vietnamese pastors sometimes treat their church members in the same way. A pastor can even eliminate a particular church member if he or she is no longer in the pastor's favor, especially those who are on the pastor's staff. Church staff and members seldom question any decisions made by their pastor regarding church activities.[22]

At this point, the reader will begin to understand the reason that the family hierarchy is important in Vietnamese culture. Vietnamese culture has been influenced by a Confucius teaching of Chinese philosophy in which children are taught to obey their parents as the rulers of the household. In the same way, in Vietnamese religious practice, church leaders have absolute power, and their practice has built a high power distance relationship between the pastor and his congregation.

Yang Liu's visual illustration excellently reflects the differences between the two cultures: East and West (See Figure 1).[23] According to western culture, an employer or manager is more or less equal to his or her employees, whereas, according to eastern culture, the employer is like an emperor. In fact, leaders or pastors within the Vietnamese churches typically practice the eastern model; they are the center of

---

[22] Michael Benge, "Vietnam: How the Communist Grinches Stole Christmas," Cited 13 March 2015. Online: http://www.frontpagemag.com/2015/michael-benge/vietnam-how-the-communist-grinches-stole-christmas/.

[23] Yang Liu, "*East Meets West: An Infographic Portrait*," Cited 9 April 2014. Online: http://bsix12.com/east-meets-west/.

the congregation.[24] The book *Cultures and Organizations*, written by Geert Hofstede, Gert Jan Hofstede, and Michael Minkov, gives the reader a fresh look at various styles of leadership from different backgrounds and cultures. In addition, the text gives the reader a better understanding of the complexity of the diverse leadership styles of different nationalities, which helps the reader to discern the origin of his or her own leadership style.[25]

Figure 1. Differing Perceptions of Leadership between East and West.

---

[24] Geert Hofstede, Gert Jan Hofstede, and Michael Minkov. *Cultures and Organizations: Intercultural Cooperation and Its Importance for Survival* (New York: McGraw Hill, 2010), 80-81.

[25] Ibid., 67-80.

VIETNAMESE PASTOR AS EMPEROR: A MENTALITY IN VIETNAMESE CHURCHES TODAY

Even though Vietnamese immigrants left Vietnam because of such persecution, their style of maintaining relationships with one another was still influenced by their lives in Vietnam. This was especially felt in the pastor's relationship with his church members, which still engendered a high power distance relationship between the pastor's family and the other families in the church.[26] As a result, the title of *pastor* continued to be beyond the average church member's imagination to attain, and the desire to become a pastor became an idol for many church members.

One reason for the major gap that exists between the position of a pastor and the position of a non-pastoral Christian is that a pastoral vocation is understood as hereditary within pastors' families, like an emperor's hereditary position, where the only prince of an emperor could follow in this position. This traditional practice was prolonged in Vietnam since it was customary for many generations prior to the communist regime, influenced by the practice of the Vietnamese Emperor Dynasties in early centuries. According to *The Ancient Civilization of Vietnam* by Huyen Van Nguyen, the constitution of Vietnam in the

---

[26] Geert Hofstede, Gert Jan Hofstede, and Michael Minkov, *Cultures and Organizations: Intercultural Cooperation and Its Importance for Survival* (New York: McGraw Hill, 2010), 58-59.

early centuries was neither democratic nor oligarchic; rather, it was an absolute monarchy where the central power was governed by the emperor and his royal class of representatives.[27] In other words, there was a great distance between the royal families and the common people because the monarchist principle established that the emperor is the son of heaven who represents God to govern the people, and therefore, the emperor is the only one who has the mandated power to rule over his people.[28]

Following this pattern, the father of a household is also considered the head of his family, and he has absolute power over his entire family, including his spouse. Each family member has a mandate to fulfill and must satisfy his or her role and bring honor and respect to the family. As the author Huyen Van Nguyen states, all of the family members and property in the household belong to the father since he is considered the representative of his entire family.[29] Because of the traditions and beliefs that were implanted in the Vietnamese people throughout centuries, when any civilian desired to approach his leader in the government or to approach a member of royalty in the imperial palace,

---

[27] Huyen Van Nguyen, *The Ancient Civilization of Vietnam* (Hanoi: The Gioi Publishers, 1995), 118.

[28] Ibid., 118.

[29] Ibid., 118.

he was required to present a precious offering to the royal emperor in order to meet with him or make a request.

Such habitual rituals were a prolonged Vietnamese practice for centuries, and this tradition became part of the Vietnamese culture. As a result, when the communist regime was established at a high power distance, precious offerings were exchanged for relationships and opportunities in order to do business during the communist period. This tradition of expected offerings in exchange for favors also affected Vietnamese churches in the hierarchy between pastoral personnel and the Christians in the congregation. Precious offerings were exchanged for relationships, and when people who had been Christians for years wanted to be involved in church leadership, they needed to plan as many meals as possible in order to please their leader before they could be selected as one of the church's leaders; this was the way to earn their leader's favor. In other words, the meals became a means of bringing two parties closer in relationship before joining into the circle of leadership. Even today, many Vietnamese pastors blindly accept such favors without any critical discernment; however, this method of identifying and selecting new leaders does not reflect a biblical perspective.

Unfortunately, from the researcher's own observation while he was serving under the Vietnamese District of the C&MA from 1989 – 2005, many Vietnamese immigrant Christians today do not apply the biblical principles of the basic foundational qualifications for becoming over-seers and deacons in a church. Many recently-ordained first-generation Vietnamese pastors fail to teach their congregations the basic quali-fications in I Timothy 3 for selecting deacons as spiritual leaders on behalf of the entire congregation. Therefore, many deacons are selected because they are favored by the congregation, and others are selected because they belong to more dominant groups within the church who have more power than those from smaller, less influential groups.

In other words, in the present researcher's own experience under the Vietnamese District in the 1990s, chosen church staff and leaders are dependent on the dominant group within a congregation, and who-ever the dominant group selects will be a staff leader for that group in the church. In addition, a high-income person or a long-time Christian who has attended the church for many years and supported the church financially would be recognized by most church members. Therefore, such a well-known person from within a particular group would nor-mally be selected as part of the church staff without any discernment in regard to his or her spiritual life or personal family life.

As a result, many Vietnamese pastors who have stepped into church ministry without proper training are heavily influenced by this dicta-torship style of leadership as they lead their own congregations.[30] Such

---

[30] Huyen Van Nguyen, *The Ancient Civilization of Vietnam* (Hanoi: The Gioi Publishers, 1995), 118

unfair and unbiblical behavior may be sabotaging the body of Christ without the pastors realizing its influence as they lead a church. For example, many Vietnamese pastors today who are leading congregations often misunderstand and misjudge the direction and vision of their younger generations, whom they expect to become very active members within a church.

Generally, the Vietnamese younger generations want to continue to follow their pastors' steps in serving the Lord, but first-generation Vietnamese leaders typically undervalue their younger generation's thoughts and ideas. The first-generation leaders are often afraid that new ideas and suggestions that come from younger generations might undermine their high power status in the church, and therefore, the voices of younger generations are seldom heard in the church, nor in any Vietnamese conference whose purpose is for the Vietnamese Christian community to learn and to share thoughts for a better spiritual community.

Another frustration, from the researcher's own observation, that prompts many younger generation or potential leaders to leave their churches is that their senior pastors frequently fail to treat the people in their congregations as their equals. Since a church typically must have a men's group, women's group, youth group, and children's group, the pastor should pray for them and bless their assigned group leaders rather than checking up on them without notice. Pastors should spend time with the church leaders and staff to develop better relationships through prayer and biblical discussion. Instead, many first-generation pastors, using their high power distance influence, interrupt their church's small groups in the middle of the meetings without informing the leaders in advance, which typically makes the younger generation and assigned leaders feel humiliated as if they have done something wrong. Because of such intergenerational cultural differences, the first-generation pastors do not realize that those in the younger generations are not familiar with these aspects of a high power distance culture, which would be easily understood by those who were fathers and children in Vietnam. The younger generations here in America want the older generation to treat them as their equals and to value their work as well. It is important to them to establish a chain of communication and trust with their leaders.

Since in Vietnamese culture and tradition a father is the head of his family, many first-generation pastors apply this mandate to their authority at church, and they expect all the church members, including the staff and assistant leaders, to show their respect through obediently following instructions instead of questioning them.[31] In the research-

---

[31] Jonathan Y. Tan, "Issues, Challenges, and Pastoral Strategies in Asian American Catholic Marriage Ministry," n.p. Cited 12 March 2015. Online: http://www.jonathantan.org/essays/INTAMS_Essay.pdf.

er's own experience under the Vietnamese District in late 1990s, a Vietnamese pastor often thinks that he can come and sit in any of his church's groups or interfere with people's discussions at any time during their meetings, since he considers himself as an overseer who has absolute power over every group in his church. Thus, he feels he has the right and authority to interfere in the activities of each group even though the groups have already selected their leaders. Many first-generation Vietnamese pastors do not realize that they are dealing with people who have been raised and have grown up in America with a different background and tradition; they are a generation of well-educated and socially-sophisticated Vietnamese-American young people.

Furthermore, many Vietnamese pastors think that a pastor's position is like an emperor who can oversee the activities of the whole church and who can make or change any rule for the entire church. As a result, first-generation Vietnamese pastors often hurt members of the Vietnamese younger generations by failing to understand their spiritual needs. Such pastors give commands for others to follow instead of listening and realizing the historical setting of their audience. First-generation Vietnamese pastors today continue to believe that they are center of their congregations, rather than a partner and co-laborer with potential leaders from within their congregations.

CULUTRAL GAP BETWEEN THE FIRST (OLDER) GENERATION AND SECOND (YOUNGER) GENERATION VIETNAMESE IN THE VIETNAMESE CHURCH IN AMERICA

Meanwhile, as the first-generation Vietnamese immigrants focused on their new jobs in order to adapt to a new environment, Vietnamese parents were happy to see the younger generation obtain the freedom to enjoy their academic life at school with great promise toward a great future. Since many young people would not have had that same freedom in Vietnam if they had continued to live under the dictatorship and religious persecution of the communists, Vietnamese parents were more than willing to sacrifice their time and their lives in order to support their children financially so that the younger Vietnamese generation would have a brighter future in America.

In working hard to support the future of the younger Vietnamese generation in America, many Vietnamese parents spent hours and hours investing their time and energy on earning income through manual labor, if necessary. The first-generation Vietnamese immigrants did not foresee the cultural gap that was gradually emerging between the Asian parents and their Vietnamese-American children in the 30 years following their resettlement in the United States. A majority of the Vietnamese parents still communicated with their children at home in Vietnamese and used their authority to give commands within the family; they did this purposefully because they did not want to see their children lose their mother-tongue. Thus, the Vietnamese family rules established by the Vietnamese parents were different from the instruction in the American classrooms, which created conflict between the Vietnamese parents and their children at home.[32]

One of the rules that Vietnamese parents often enforce while they are raising their children at home is to have them concentrate on their studies almost 24 hours a day in order to bring home an "A" grade instead of a "B" grade. Furthermore, even if children bring home all "A's" in class, their parents would encourage their children to bring home an "A+" instead. In fact, since Vietnamese culture and belief are highly influenced by Confucianism, which stresses respect for educated people, immigrant parents generally consider their children's education as a top priority.[33]

In addition, according to Pang and Cheng in *Struggling to be Heard*, Asian parents are largely willing to sacrifice their time and strength at work in return for their children's educational success. With such high expectations, immigrant parents continually encourage their children to endure hardships and persevere to achieve high grades and

---

[32] Christin McKarthy, "Adaptation of Immigrant Children to United States: A Review of the Literature," n.p. Cited 13 march 2015. Online: http://crcw.princeton.edu/workingpapers/WP98-03-McCarthy.pdf.

[33] Eun Young Kim, Career Choice Among Second Generation Korean Americans: Reflections of Cultural Model of Success. *Anthropology and Education Quarterly*, 24, 224-248.

academic success and to make themselves mentally stronger.[34] Asian parents aspire for their children's success to make the entire family proud of what their children have accomplished in front of the parents' relatives as well as in public.

In other words, Vietnamese children felt extreme pressure regarding their studies because they were pressed to be the top students in order to satisfy their parents as well as to give their parents a reason to be proud among their Vietnamese neighbors. Because of the divergent perspectives between what the Vietnamese parents and the younger generation were looking for in daily life, communication between the Vietnamese parents and their children often resulted in conflict. Both parties were coming from different perspectives, and such conflict had rarely appeared prior to this time between the two generations in the home. The first-generation of Vietnamese parents often believe that they have the right to stop their children's conversation at any point without a reasonable explanation, and the children must show their submission at any time without a word of explanation because their parents are the decision-makers; Vietnamese parents believe that their decision-making is in the best interests of their children.

---

[34] Valerie Ooka Pang and Li-Rong Lilly Cheng, eds., *Struggling to Be Heard: The Unmet Needs of Asian Pacific American Children* (Albany: State University of New York, 1998), 98.

Vietnamese parents did not realize that their children were growing up in a different culture, and their concepts regarding church and people were quite different than an Asian perspective. For a variety of reasons, this resulted in a change in the relationships between immigrant parents and children. Since Vietnamese children are born or raised in America, they have better language skills and more opportunities as a result of their education; in addition, children of Vietnamese immigrants are more familiar with western cultural norms than their immigrant parents.

Thus, to use Hofstede's observations regarding individualism and collectivism,[35] the younger-generation Vietnamese have been influenced to be independent according to the western culture in which individualism is highly promoted. In contrast, in their homes, a majority of the younger generation Vietnamese are still strongly under the influence of the traditional family values of collectivism and family hierarchy.[36]

This widening social and generational gap was also happening within the Vietnamese immigrant churches in America, where immigrant parents considered attending church as part of a cultural tradition instead of as a way of supporting their children to grow spiritually.

---

[35] Geert Hofsted, Gert Jan Hofstede and Michael Minkov, *Cultures and Organizations: Software of the Mind-Intercultural Cooperation and Its Importance for Survival* (New York: McGraw Hill, 2010), 129.

[36] Ibid., 129.

In the same way that immigrant parents use their authority to force their children to focus on academic achievement, the church environment and its culture are also built on that basic tradition wherein the first-generation pastors, considered as the heads of each church, seem to believe that they have absolute power to make decisions on behalf of their congregations.

As a result, a conflict of communication inevitably happens between the first-generation pastors and the potential leaders from the younger generation because the first-generation church leaders cannot communicate effectively with the young people to discuss their problems and give guidance. The second generation of leaders lacks support both from church leaders and the church congregations.[37] In fact, tension often occurs between parents and children and between pastors and younger potential leaders due to intergenerational gaps and the inclination of adolescent children and young adults in immigrant families to reject traditional Vietnamese values in favor of American values.[38]

Additional examples related to the Vietnamese church setting also demonstrate how the younger Asian generations today think differently from their Asian parents. When a potential young leader is assigned a

---

[37] Eunice Or, "Supporting Second Generation Church Leaders: Understanding and Mentorship to Support Second Generation Church Leaders," n.p. Cited 30 January 2015. Online: http://l2foundation.org/2007/supporting-second-generation-church-leaders.

[38] Presentation, "Asian American Cultural Awareness," n.p. Cited 4 November 2014. Online: http://www.cedu.niu.edu/~shumow/itt/Asian_American_Cultural_Awareness.pdf.

certain responsibility in the church or home, he or she will ordinarily accomplish the assigned task successfully, but parents or pastors rarely extend their gratitude for the completed task; this makes the younger person feel embarrassed and unappreciated. Even though the younger generations are not looking for others to see them as heroes, they at least would like others to acknowledge the task that they have carried out successfully.

The Vietnamese immigrant church community is not the only Asian immigrant population to be experiencing intergenerational challenges. According to an Asian-American Reporter's Conference in regard to Asian-American churches facing a leadership gap, a 2005 Duke Divinity School study "Asian American Religious Leadership Today" said the "most acute tensions" in Asian American churches revolved around two issues:[39]

1. Continual clashes between the generations over cultural differences in the styles and philosophies of church leadership and control.

2. Young pastors' view that immigrant churches are "dysfunctional and hypocritical religious institutions" that demonstrate a "negative expression" of Christian spirituality for the second generation.

---

[39] K. Connie Kang, "Asian American churches face leadership gap," n.p. *LA Times*. (March 03rd, 2007). Cited 30 January 2015. Online: http://articles.latimes.com/2007/mar/03/local/me-beliefs3.

The above study conducted by Duke Divinity School identifies perhaps one of the most significant generational conflicts within the Vietnamese churches in America today, which is the lack of valuation of the second generation Vietnamese.

Such cross-cultural differences in values were not the only challenge between the Vietnamese immigrant parents and their children; other cultural clashes occurred within the Vietnamese churches in the United States. An additional example will demonstrate that cultural differences can even bring greater discontent and alienation to the Vietnamese immigrant churches. For example, for Sunday worship in Vietnamese churches, the sermon is the central focus of the service. Announcements and choir songs are a part of the service, but they are considered a much less significant part than the sermon. This is one of the ways that first-generation pastors and parents have maintained their cultural church practices from Vietnam in their new churches in America, without taking into consideration that their children do not understand their purpose for attending church every Sunday. Furthermore, the Vietnamese younger generation views their Vietnamese Sunday service as a place for traditional and habitual performances instead of a place to worship God; thus, the first and second generation cultures clash in their worship styles, leadership styles, and so on.[40]

---

[40] Shiao Chong, "Church and Culture," n.p. Cited 4 November 2014. Online: http://3dchristianity.wordpress.com/2012/02/03/church-and-culture/.

Since the first-generation pastors and parents believe that the Sunday service must include a sermon monologue preached only by the pastor, any alternate ideas, such as a musical play with biblical characters based on Scripture, are still considered as secondary activities which are only appropriate for camp participation outside the main church service. Whenever there is an approach from anyone in the younger generation addressing their interest in serving alongside pastors or in changing the service style to better meet their spiritual needs, the first-generation pastors are commonly reluctant to allow such implementations to occur because they believe that preaching a monologue in the pulpit cannot be replaced by any other type of Bible presentation. Thus, most of the suggestions and ideas from younger people will be immediately rejected by the first-generation pastors because their sermon must be preached; the teaching cannot occur in any other form. As a result, many of the first-generation Vietnamese in America today face the challenge of seeing the younger generation leaving their parents' churches because of the unwillingness of the first-generation leaders to see and respond to the needs of the rising generations in the Vietnamese immigrant churches in America.

The fundamental reason that first-generation Vietnamese pastors have maintained the traditional way of worship and monologue preaching onstage for more than three decades in America is that they believe that contemporary worship and preaching styles are not faithful ways to serve the Lord. As a result, the first-generation Vietnamese pastors would rather re-live the past by reinforcing past practices and ideals that they still remember—instead of acknowledging the spiritual needs of the rising generations and helping them to map out their spiritual paths based on Scripture.

In the meantime, since many first-generation Vietnamese pastors do not acknowledge that their traditional concepts are different from the second generation's concepts, the first-generation Vietnamese pastors often ignore this intergenerational gap and the generational cultural shift within their churches. Instead of supporting the younger generations within a congregation to experience God's call and then encouraging those potential leaders to attend seminary for further training, the Vietnamese first-generation pastors instead welcomed others from the first generation who wanted to step into leadership as pastors, either to replace a retired pastor or to assign them to other churches being planted in other locations.

This practice of choosing co-workers from other first-generation Vietnamese churches, which commonly occurred between 1998 and 2012, according to the researcher's own observation, revealed that the first-generation Vietnamese pastors did not value their potential young leaders who were raised in the United States. The first-generation pastors would only select others from the first generation within the Vietnamese churches and quickly ordain them as pastors, which soon became the standard practice among the Vietnamese churches during this period. The qualifications for a person from the first generation to become a pastor did not necessarily include being a graduate of a seminary; rather, he might be accepted as a pastor solely through his church supporting his desire to be a pastor. Furthermore, since any person from the first generation could easily enter into ministry at a church, the first-generation Vietnamese pastors preferred to use this method to replace aging pastors within the Vietnamese church nationwide.

This practice created a greater gap between the first and the second generations due to their different ideas and the language barrier between the two generations under one church roof. In addition, from the researcher's own observation, since obtaining a pastoral title or role was so easy for the first-generation pastors, a majority of the first-generation pastors thought that simply gaining this title was adequate preparation for leading others; however, none of them had been trained in the leadership skills necessary to prepare them for a spiritual vocation in the church.

Welcoming second-generation men and women into church leadership and training them to become effective pastors is an absolute necessity if current young leaders are truly discerning God's calling for them to enter into such a vocation. Recruiting first-generation immigrants who were called to church leadership into pastoral roles was a good way to meet the needs of the fast-growing Vietnamese population in the late 2000s; however, preparing young men and woman for the pastoral ministry to meet the spiritual needs of the younger generation and engaging these younger potential leaders into the church's ministry are still missing components of the leadership development process.

One of the biggest tragedies happening in the Vietnamese churches today is that often first-generation pastors typically do not want to step down when they reach retirement age, and therefore, many Vietnamese churches are filled with aging leaders and no younger, well-trained successors as ministers. The records in the National Office of the C&MA reflect that the majority of pastors who serve under the Vietnamese District are 50 years old or older. Very few were born after 1970; thus, all of them were born or mostly raised in Vietnam. There are essentially no American-born pastors in the Vietnamese District.[41] Shockingly, there have been no new churches planted by the second generation of Vietnamese leaders after nearly forty years under the Vietnamese District of the C&MA, according to one of the latest reports in *Hoi*

---

[41] "Vietnamese Church Annual Report" (excel spread sheet, National Office of The Christian and Missionary Alliance, n.d.). Received with permission for this dissertation on 18 March 2015.

Thanh Ta assembled by Rev. Ba Quang Nguyen, the former Vietnamese district superintendent of C&MA.[42]

A recent census report from 2010 shows that the Vietnamese-American population has reached 1,548,449; this number can be used to put in perspective the number of Vietnamese Protestants in the United States today.[43] According to a comprehensive, nationwide survey of Asian Americans conducted by the Pew Research Center, Vietnamese Asian-Americans who consider themselves Protestant make up the smallest population in comparison to other populations of Protestants from other Asian nationalities in America.[44] In fact, only 6 percent of the Vietnamese-American population is comprised of Vietnamese Protestants, compared to 36 percent of Catholic Christians and 43 percent of Buddhists, with the remaining 20 percent as unaffiliated (See Figure 2). The above statistics show only that the Vietnamese church in America is small compared to other groups, but there is no accurate

---

[42] Nguyen Ba Quang, *Hội Thánh Ta* (Hội Thánh Tin Lành Việt Nam – Giáo Hạt Việt Nam Hoa Kỳ-Fullerton, California: 2000), 1.

[43] United States Census Bureau, "The Vietnamese Population in the United States: 2010," n.p. Cited 30 January 2015. Online: http://www.bpsos.org/mainsite/images/DelawareValley/community_profile/us.census.2010.the%20vietnamese%20population_july%202.2011.pdf.

[44] Pew Research Center, "Asian Americans: A Mosaic of Faiths," n.p. Cited 30 January 2015. Online: http://www.pewforum.org/2012/07/19/asian-americans-a-mosaic-of-faiths-overview/.

data on the percentage of second-generation Vietnamese Americans who attend church.[45]

According to Pyong Gap Min, a study of second-generation Korean Americans reflects that only 5 percent of the second generation remains in the church after college while up to 75 percent of the first generation attends church. This information supports the researcher's supposition that because of different worldviews between Korean parents and Korean-American children born or raised in America, Korean young people who are eighteen and older had a tendency to want to escape their parents in order to avoid their parents' complaints about their disrespectful behavior and talking back.[46]

---

[45] Linh Hoang, "The Faith and Practice of Asian American Catholics: Generational Shifts," n.p. Cited 13 March 2015. Online: https://www.mysciencework.com/publication/file/1396321/the-faith-and-practice-of-asian-american-catholics-generational-shifts.

[46] Pyong Gap Min, *Changes and Conflicts: Korean Immigrant Families in New York* (Boston, MA: Allyn and Bacon, 1997), 199.

Religious Affiliation of Asian-American Subgroups

Chinese Americans

- All Christian 31%
- Protestant 22%
- Unaffiliated 52%
- Catholic 8%
- Buddhist 15%

Filipino Americans

- Buddhist 1%
- Unaffiliated 8%
- All Christian 89%
- Protestant 21%
- Catholic 65%

Indian Americans

- Jain 2%
- Sikh 5%
- Unaffiliated 10%
- Protestant 11%
- All Christian 18%
- Catholic 5%
- Muslim 10%
- Hindu 51%

Vietnamese Americans

- Prot. 6%
- All Christian 36%
- Unaffiliated 20%
- Catholic 30%
- Buddhist 43%

Korean Americans

- All Christian 71%
- Unaffiliated 23%
- Buddhist 6%
- Catholic 10%
- Protestant 61%

Japanese Americans

- All Christian 38%
- Unaffiliated 32%
- Protestant 33%
- Other 4%
- Buddhist 25%
- Cath. 4%

The "All Christian" category includes Protestants, Catholics and other Christians. Subgroups are listed in order of the size of the country-of-origin group in the total Asian-American population. Those who did not give an answer are not shown. Other religion, Hindu and Buddhist not shown for some subgroups. See topline in Appendix 4 for all responses.

PEW RESEARCH CENTER

Figure 2. Religious affiliation of Asian-American population

To respond to the facts reports by the Pew Research Center, the population of Vietnamese Christians nationwide is likely decreasing even though the Vietnamese churches have been established for nearly forty years in America. The Pew Research Center does not reflect a decreased number of Vietnamese Protestants in any particular denomination, such as the Vietnamese district of the C&MA, but its results reflect the total number of all Protestants, including Vietnamese C&MA, Vietnamese Baptist, Vietnamese Methodist, Vietnamese Presbyterian, and other evangelical denominations in the United States.

STATEMENT OF THE MINISTRY PROBLEM

Even though Vietnamese churches have been established in America since the early 1980s, the younger generations of Vietnamese who are born and grow up in America are not significantly involved in the leadership of their local churches. Most of the Vietnamese church administration and activities are run by pastors or leaders for as long as they can until they retire. The researcher conducted a telephone conversation with one of the church elders at the Vietnamese church in Atlanta, Georgia, in regard to the reasons that many Vietnamese young people are not actively involved at their local church. The response reveals that the younger people feel alienated from the church since the church practices traditions of a culture of which they are not really a part.[47] The younger generation Vietnamese look at their heritage churches as cultural clubs where their parents come for a reminder of their past that was grounded in their regular church service.[48] This philosophy hinders the progress of the church instead of allowing opportunity to seek an appropriate model for church administration and leadership development. In other words, cultural and generational bias typically becomes a stumbling block for younger generations to succeed in ministry.

Another outdated practice within the Vietnamese church today is the Sunday worship agenda. The first-generation members are typically interested in the old songs composed in the early 1920s, which have little rhythm or joyfulness. The younger generation cannot understand the words that are sung from the Vietnamese hymn books because they are written in an older Vietnamese script which contains metaphorical meanings that are unfamiliar to the younger generation. In addition, they do not appreciate the rhythm which comes with a slow melody and is full of sadness instead of joy. These traditional practices that are preserved within the church create miscommunication and misunderstanding between the first and the second generations.

---

[47] Linh Hoang, "The Faith and Practice of Asian American Catholics: Generational Shifts," n.p. Cited 13 March 2015. Online: https://www.mysciencework.com/publication/file/1396321/the-faith-and-practice-of-asian-american-catholics-generational-shifts.

[48] Ibid., no pages.

Unfortunately, a majority of the Vietnamese pastors and leaders today are reluctant to engage their potential younger leaders in church activities, especially in church worship and administration. Instead, in many ways, the church leaders distance themselves from the younger generation and assert that the younger people should observe and obey instead of criticize. Among the Vietnamese churches, the researcher's own observations also reveal that church pastors and leaders often assume that the younger people should volunteer to work for the church without any compensation until the whole congregation or church staff considers their contributions to be beneficial and believes that they should become paid employees. In *Supporting Second Generation Church Leaders*, Eunice Or cites Lee as saying that even when Chinese churches have welcomed second-generation Chinese ministers, these leaders have encountered many obstacles when working with first-generation overseas-born Chinese leaders because of the differences in culture.[49] Likewise, dialogue between the first and the second generation is also rare within the Vietnamese church, where the first-generation Vietnamese often think that their role is to lead the church and to provide for the church financially as well as to make decisions regarding the direction of the church—without involvement from the younger generation.

---

[49] Eunice Or, "Supporting Second Generation Church Leaders: Understanding and Mentorship to Support Second Generation Church Leaders," n.p. Cited 30 January 2015. Online: http://l2foundation.org/2007/supporting-second-generation-church-leaders.

In addition, Christian leaders, according to the Asian-American conference, report that Asian-American churches are going through a "crisis of leadership" because there is no one from the younger generation willing to enter seminaries for training. For instance, Rev. Sang Hyun Lee from Princeton Theological Seminary in New Jersey indicates that the number of Asian American students was down to about 50 from more than 100 in the 1990s.[50] Fumitaka Matsuoka, a former dean of the Pacific School of Religion at Berkeley, also claimed that there are not many students responding to the seminary program even though the school offers generous financial aid.[51]

This tragedy of the separation between the first and second generations of an immigrant community does not only happen within the Vietnamese immigrant churches in the United States. Korean immigrant churches also experience similar challenges as they have not been able to achieve a common understanding between the old and the young generations. In fact, when the second-generation of Koreans became adults, a conflict arose between the two generations, which was viewed as a "lack of ideological vision" within both generations.[52]

---

[50] K. Connie Kang, "Asian American Churches Face Leadership Gap," n.p. Cited 30 January 2015. Online: http://articles.latimes.com/2007/mar/03/local/me-beliefs3.

[51] Ibid., no pages.

[52] Sejong Chun. *Galatians and Korean Immigrants*. p. 3.

A similar scenario also occurred within the immigrant population from India, according to Ashish Raichur, in his article *The Second Generation: Spiritual and Cultural Conflict*. Raichur accurately identifies the same problem within the Indian churches in America, which is that church leaders have failed to provide for the spiritual needs of the second generation, resulting in a major gap between the two groups; thus, the younger generation typically does not like to attend their parents' churches. The church typically becomes a gathering location for social forums and cultural activities for those in the first generation to live in their past.[53]

Chinese churches in America also face the same problem of failing to recognize the need for the first generation to support the second generation within church. Instead of being concerned for the spiritual growth of the second-generation Chinese, church leaders and parents have overemphasized the children's academic achievements and disregarded other needs.[54] Furthermore, Eunice Or strongly calls out to the first-generation leaders in Chinese churches to show tolerance to the younger generation as well as to humble themselves to support and to serve their younger

---

[53] Ashish Raichur, "The Second Generation: Spiritual and Cultural Conflicts" *Agape Partners International*. n.p. Cited on 5th November 2014. Online: http://agapepartners. org/articles/34/1/The-Second-GenerationSpiritual-and-Cultural-Conflicts/Page1.html. .

[54] Eunice Or, "Supporting Second Generation Church Leaders," n.p. Cited 4 November 2014. Online: http://l2foundation.org/2007/supporting-second-generation-church-leaders.

generation according to God's will instead of traditionally protecting leadership roles among themselves.[55]

As seen from the preceding paragraphs, the Asian immigrant churches, including the Vietnamese churches, are no exception to the struggles between generations. In fact, most of the Vietnamese pastors in the United States seem to be overlooking the fact that the Vietnamese churches in America will soon have to address the post-modernist Vietnamese generation that is arising. These young people have grown up in a free country with no experience of religious persecution and instead have had to confront moral issues, capitalism, and individualism. At a result, the second-generation Vietnamese have prioritized a focus on secular professions to meet their economic needs instead of considering entering seminaries for spiritual vocational training.[56]

THEOLOGICAL FOUNDATIONS THEORETICAL APPROACHES TO RETENTION AND LEADERSHIP DEVELOPMENT OF THE YOUNGER GENERATION

Because of the Vietnamese cultural mindset, even though the Vietnamese churches had successfully multiplied and planted many additional churches in the U.S. through the efforts of pastors and

---

[55] Eunice Or, no pages.

[56] K. Connie Kang, "Asian American Churches Face Leadership Gap," n.p. Cited 30 January 2015. Online: http://articles.latimes.com/2007/mar/03/local/me-beliefs3.

newly recruited co-workers from the first generation, a majority of the Vietnamese churches in America are still influenced by a dictatorship style of leadership where pastors often hold absolute power. In other words, like people in many societies, they are hungry to establish their identities within their own social settings to achieve power.[57] Unfortunately, in this case, the cultural mindset of the first generation of Vietnamese leaders is in many ways contradictory to the teaching of Scripture.

The biblical mandate and the practical application of making disciples are essential within the local church. However, defining styles of leadership and identifying the process by which the development of spiritual leaders should take place need to emerge as topics of discussion. Leadership itself has been described in many ways. There are many experiences and methodologies that have been published by church pioneers, helping followers to discern problematic issues and to prepare to deal with the concerns of the church, including the declining attendance in recent decades. Research has identified eight elements of leadership style that are necessary to yield a high rate of retention of the second generation; these elements may particularly helpful for consideration within the Vietnamese churches nationwide

---

[57] Geert Hofsted, Gert Jan Hofstede and Michael Minkov, *Cultures and Organizations: Software of the Mind-Intercultural Cooperation and Its Importance for Survival* (New York: McGraw Hill, 2010), 20.

to increase retention of the second generation of Vietnamese. It is vital for Vietnamese pastors to begin to wrestle with these elements for the benefit of their churches.

The concept of servant leadership is one of the elements that might help the first-generation Vietnamese pastors today to achieve success in yielding a high rate of second-generation retention in the local church. As a leader of a church, a pastor must face many challenges in order to serve effectively among church members. There will be many differing opinions and ideas that people will expect their pastors to incorporate in order to make the church satisfy the needs of the people in the congregation. Therefore, without a heart for humbly serving others, a pastor is likely to get into confrontations with people instead of serving them. James Means, in *Leadership in Christian Ministry*, expresses that if pastors and leaders believe that they are placed in unquestioned authority over the members, then confrontation and division will likely exist because these types of leaders often believe that they are the primary liaisons between God and the church members.[58] Means also said that pastors who have this kind of mindset usually believe that they are in charge of those below them, and, therefore, they behave like the head of the church.[59] An alternative way for leaders and pastors to lead

---

[58] James E. Means, *Leadership in Christian Ministry*, Foreword by Kenneth O. Gangel (Grand Rapids, Michigan, Baker Book House, 1989), 43.

[59] James E. Means, 44.

a church successfully, according to James Means' solution, is to treat others as colleagues, not as subordinates.[60]

Another definition of humility for leaders and pastors as they serve among church members, according to Mike Yaconelli in his *Core Realities of Youth Ministry: Nine Biblical Principles that Mark Healthy Youth Ministry*, is to be gentle, meek, not arrogant, unassuming, unpretentious, kind, unassertive, and quiet.[61] Because of their cultural backgrounds, it is very difficult for the first generation of Vietnamese pastors to think of humility as a positive value. However, biblically, humility is presented as a positive characteristic of a leader. Yaconelli states that many Christians misunderstand humility. They view it as a socially desirable quality, and lip service is paid to the value of humility, but in truth, humility is not valued in many cultures.[62] Another aspect of Yaconelli's description of what a humble leader looks like would challenge many Asian leaders, especially the first generation of Vietnamese pastors and leaders. This aspect highlights the importance of recognizing that every person is fallible, and thus, pastors and leaders need to depend heavily on God and to become teachable instead of basing their decisions upon cultural values and traditions. In other words, pastors

---

[60] Ibid., 44.

[61] Mike Yaconelli, the *Core Relalities of Youth Monistry: Nine Biblical Principles that Mark Healthy Youth Ministry* (Grand Rapids, Michigan: Zondervan, 2003), 63.

[62] Ibid., 65.

and leaders need to increase their knowledge, to change their behavior, to adapt to the needs of the younger generation, and to restructure the church environment.[63]

In *Humble Leadership* by N. Graham Standish, the author clearly describes that there are at least two steps for helping pastors and leaders develop a humble effective leadership style. The first step is rooted in prayer because prayer is a time to give God a chance to speak to his people.[64] The second step is to show a willingness to remain open to the power and the leading of the work of the Holy Spirit.[65] Without the above steps of exhibiting a heart of willingness to wait for and to hear for God's voice through daily prayer and meditation, pastors are not preparing themselves adequately in advance to reflect Christ-likeness as they serve among their church congregations.

Another practical procedure for helping pastors and leaders to become humble servants in order to lead God's sheep successfully is for them to train their state of mind. This requires years of learning to walk daily with God through meditation, as well as to work patiently with one another within the church staff and members. In *The Leadership Ellipse* by Robert A. Fryling, the author states that pastors and church

---

[63] Mike Yaconelli, 67.

[64] N. Graham Standish, *Humble Leadership: Being Radically Open to God's Guidance and Grace*, Foreword by Diana Butler Bass (Herndon, Virginia: The Alban Institute), 62.

[65] Ibid., 125.

leaders need to embrace the practice of humble thought, where pastors need to renew their minds by pursuing and receiving the quiet work of God's Spirit within the core of their beings.[66] In other words, resisting the influence of worldly temptations and evil thought is not enough; they must actively respond with a desire to maintain a relationship with God through reading Scripture and communicating through prayer in order to renew their spiritual minds.

Dan Reiland, in *Amplified Leadership*, recommends that pastors and leaders need to invite individuals into meaningful ministry by which people's lives will be changed.[67] In other words, pastors and leaders need to be examples of treating others as their equals and should seek a godly cultural development wherein younger generations, especially potential leaders, will learn how to serve and to live in a godly way.

David F. Nixon, in *Leading the Comeback Church*, explains that pastors and leaders should serve as a connection between God and their congregations, and thus, like Christ himself, pastors and leaders are like carpenters, and they need to treat others as their equals in order to pick up their tools together to become bridge-builders.[68] In fact, part of

---

[66] Robert A. Fryling, *The Leadership Ellipse: Shaping How We Lead by Who We Are*, Foreword by Eugene H. Peterson (Downer Grove, Illinois: IVP Books, 2010), 66.

[67] Dan Reiland, *Amplified Leadership: Five Practices to Establish Influence, Build People, and Impact Othes for a Lifetime*, Forward by John C. Maxwell (Lake Mary, Florida: Charisma House Book Goup, 2011), 87.

[68] David F. Nixon, *Leading the Comeback Church: Help Your Church Rebound from Decline* (Kansas City, Missouri:Beacon Hill Press of Kansas City, 2004), 144.

the church vocation is God's call for leaders to seek to involve every believer in God's work, and thus, a person called into ministry should not ignore others but should value them and multiply them as godly workers for Christ.

SERVANT LEADERSHIP STYLE DEFINED IN SCRIPTURE

Recruiting and training young potential leaders within a local church is not a common practice among many first-generation Vietnamese churches in America. The reader can find many practical examples of how Jesus lived in his three and a half years of ministry on earth among his people. Jesus successfully portrayed a picture of how a spiritual servant leader should act among others in order to fulfill his Great Commission. There are at least five elements that Jesus lived out as an example of a servant leadership model before his disciples.

According to Matthew 9:35, "when he traveled through all the cities and villages of that area, Jesus saw the multitude and he had compassion on them because they were harassed and helpless, like sheep without a shepherd." In other words, the heart of a servant leader is one that can see the needs of the people, and Jesus clearly demonstrated that leadership element, which should serve as motivation for a servant leader to focus on this element as well. The second element in a servant leadership model is demonstrated by Jesus when he went by himself to a mountain to pray to God all night before he called all of his disciples the next day and chose them to be apostles (Lk. 6:12-13). During his time on earth, Jesus unfailingly maintained his primary relationship with God the Father before he began to do things for others; this is a characteristic that godly servant leaders would do well to emulate.

The third element for a servant leadership model is availability: Jesus made himself personally available to anyone who needed access to him. According to Mark, when parents brought their children to Jesus so he could bless them, Jesus' disciples tried to block them, and they did not allow them to approach Jesus (Mk.10:13-15). However, Jesus was displeased with his disciples and said to them, "Let the children come to me. Don't stop them." Jesus has perfectly set himself as an example of a servant leader by demonstrating the compassion to serve others.

The fourth element of a servant leadership model was evident when Jesus patiently spent his time to explain and interpret his message regarding the kingdom of God to his own disciples by using parables when they did not really understand his preaching about his heavenly kingdom (Matt.13: 1-23). In other words, Jesus portrayed himself as a model of a servant leader so that his disciples would be able to learn much more about the Great Commission that Jesus had revealed to the world.

The last, but not least, element Jesus displayed in his public ministry as a servant leader was caring for people's physical needs. According to Matthew 14: 14-21, after a day of traveling, Jesus knew that he and his disciples were tired and hungry, as were the multitudes who followed him. Jesus felt compassion for them, and he asked his disciples to buy food to feed this multitude. Furthermore, according to John's gospel, at one time after Jesus' resurrection, Peter and a few other disciples went together to catch fish at the Sea of Galilee, but they got nothing for their work that night. Jesus stood on the shore and he told them to try again to catch some fish. This time, he directed them exactly how to do it (Jn. 21: 1-8). Jesus perfectly represented himself as the model of a servant leader with a godly character; in this particular scenario, when he saw such discouragement among his own disciples, he continued to reveal who he was, instead of reflecting an irritable attitude toward his disciples.

As seen from these examples, Jesus consistently demonstrated godly qualities of an effective spiritual leader while he was living and preaching among the people; he showed how to preach the good news of the kingdom and how to prepare followers to be sent out with God's Great Commission to bring many more lost people into His kingdom. Ironically, Vietnamese pastors and church leaders have typically overlooked Jesus' style of teaching and have neglected to demonstrate

Christ-likeness as an example for others due to the historical influence of patriarchy. Tradition appears to exert a stronger influence than accurate biblical teaching. The characteristics of the traditional pastoral role have been rooted for many generations within the Vietnamese culture and have made older Vietnamese pastors and church leaders reluctant to challenge or change those roles.[69]

Since culture is man-made and is comprised of the characteristics and knowledge of a particular group or tribe of people, it can be very difficult to change because it reflects the spectrum of values and beliefs of each nationality—including the characteristics of the religions within that culture.[70] However, Jesus himself was counter-cultural and established a new example for his disciples to follow in order to overcome man-made culture when he pronounced that the kingdom of God had arrived (Lk. 17:21 KJV). In other words, Jesus laid down his life as a servant to go and seek the lost, to heal the sick, and to bring the good news of the kingdom of God to everybody. In addition, Jesus himself set aside time with his disciples where he taught them to spend time praying to God the Father, which gave him the strength to overcome all kinds of persecution.

---

[69] Monica McGoldrick, Randy Gerson, and Sueli Petry, *Genograms: Assessment and Intervention* (3rd ed. New York, NY: W.W. Norton Company, 2007), 37.

[70] Kim Ann Zimmerman, "What is Culture? Definition of Culture," n.p. *Live Science Contributor.* Cited 31 March 2015. Online: http://www.livescience.com/21478-what-is-culture-definition-of-culture.html.

Essentially, Jesus set an example among his disciples in order to train his followers to adopt a new way of life within the kingdom of God, by establishing relationships in which a servant leader serves others starting from a loving heart instead of a love of his position, as Jesus demonstrated when he rebuked his disciples, the two sons of Zebedee, who hoped to sit in places of honor (Matt. 20: 24-28). A relevant practice for today's pastors and church leaders would be to overcome some unproductive aspects of their man-made cultures in order to experience God's kingdom on earth as Christ himself typified during his entire ministry before his ascension. In other words, current relationships with one another should be transformed for a more productive future.[71]

The Apostle Paul also emphasizes in his teaching that when people accept Christ as their Savior, they are entering into a new life in Christ because the blood of Christ has cleansed their sins, and as new believers, they become God's children. Therefore, Christians should learn how to live out this new life by giving their bodies to God as living sacrifices, holy and pleasing to God (Rom. 12:1). In fact, without giving up their bodies as living sacrifices to God in daily life, Christians cannot empty themselves in order to serve others as Christ's servant leaders, according to Paul's teaching in Philippians 2:5-8. Again, it is essential

---

[71] Monica McGoldrick, Randy Gerson, and Sueli Petry, *Genograms: Assessment and Intervention* (3rd ed. New York, NY: W.W. Norton Company, 2007), 240.

for those who desire to serve God to overcome the unscriptural aspects of man-made cultures; this is especially true for pastors and church leaders because they are Christ's exemplars, and they should live in Christ-likeness in order to lead and to train others in accordance with Paul's teaching (II Cor. 5:20).

ASSUMPTIONS

The researcher acknowledges that the significance of the results of this study will be based on several assumptions. As with any research involving individual people, there is generally the underlying understanding that each person is unique and that there are multiple complex factors at work. In this current study of the factors that may contribute to whether or not a given participant remains in the Vietnamese church, the researcher has attempted minimize the potential for the results to be skewed by individual variations by using a relatively large sample of participants (50 in each of the three groups).

A second assumption in this study is that the three sample groups are reasonably similar in every respect except in their decision to remain in the Vietnamese church (Group A), leave the Vietnamese church to attend a non-Vietnamese church (Group B), or leave the church altogether (Group C). Given this assumption and considering the list of issues presented, if a given behavior or attitude is present in the retained group (Group A), but is absent in the non-retained groups (Group B and C), then that issue may be considered to have had some effect on retention. In other words, the relationship between that particular issue and retention may be also be considered more than merely coincidental.

THE MODEL AND PURPOSE OF THE RESEARCH

In light of the preceding observations, the present researcher decided to "test" whether a certain set of conditions related to the Vietnamese churches and their leaders were valued by second-generation Vietnamese congregants and potential church leaders and to determine whether these conditions factored into the retention or attrition of young people in the churches. A survey was created to examine the following seven issues:

- Issue 1: Whether second-generation congregants were included in performing tasks in the Sunday worship service.[72]

- Issue 2: Whether second-generation congregants believed their involvement in church events was valued.[73]

---

[72] Joan Huyser-Honig, "Nine Tips for Designing Intergenerational Worship," n.p. Cited 25 February 2015. Online: http://worship.calvin.edu/resources/resource-library/nine-tips-for-designing-intergenerational-worship/

[73] Jerry Z. Park and Joshua Tom, "Keeping (and Losing) Faith, the Asian American Way," n.p. Cited 25 February 2015. Online: http://aapivoices.com/keeping-losing-faith/.

- Issue 3: Whether second-generation congregants believed their leadership abilities were valued.[74]

- Issue 4: Whether second-generation congregants believed it was easy for them to talk to first-generation church leaders about their spiritual needs.[75]

- Issue 5: Whether second-generation congregants believed they were treated as equals by first-generation church leaders.[76]

- Issue 6: Whether second-generation congregants could relate to the vision of the church for reaching Vietnamese for Christ.[77]

- Issue 7: Whether second-generation congregants had a pastor devoted to English-speaking ministries.[78]

The researcher devised a survey to administer to second-generation Vietnamese Christians who had attended a Vietnamese church for at least two years. These participants were divided into three categories: (a) those who had remained in the Vietnamese Church, (b) those

---

[74] Peter Cha, Steve Kang and Helen Lee, eds., *Growing Healthy Asian American Churches: Ministry Insights from Groundbreaking Congregations* (Downers Grove, IL: InterVarsity Press, 2006), 60.

[75] Joseph M. Stowell, *Shepherding the Church: Effective Spiritual Leadership in a Changing Culture* (Chicago: Moody Press, 1997), 177-178.

[76] Sharon Kim, *A Faith of Our Own: Second-Generation Spirituality in Korean American Churches* (Piscataway, NJ: Rutgers University Press, 2010), 1.

[77] Peter Cha, Steve Kang and Helen Lee, eds., *Growing Healthy Asian American Churches: Ministry Insights from Groundbreaking Congregations*, (Downers Grove, IL: InterVarsity Press, 2006), 90.

[78] Peter Ong, "Exist Wounds: The Flight of Asian American Faith," n.p. Cited 25 February 2015. Online: https://peterong.wordpress.com/2006/10/20/exit-wounds-the-flight-of-asian-american-faith-published/.

who had left the Vietnamese Church and now attend a non-Vietnamese Church, and (c) those who had left church altogether. The expected outcome of the study was that differences in responses between the three groups would indicate if one or more of the issues listed above correlated to whether second-generation Vietnamese left or remained in the church.

This research is a Model 1 project, or descriptive research. It seeks to describe the state of things; nevertheless, the researcher is postulating a cause (a low sense of valuation) and an effect (a low rate of retention). While the data may show areas where Vietnamese church leaders should perhaps intervene to enhance retention, the present project will not attempt any such intervention and makes no claim to have enhanced retention.

HYPOTHESIS

The researcher hypothesized that there is a relationship between second generation leaders' sense of valuation by first-generation leaders and their retention in the Vietnamese church in America. Issues #2 through #6 will likely provide the researcher with information to confirm or contradict this hypothesis. Issues #2, #3, and #5 will speak directly to the hypothesis and will indicate whether the involvement and leadership abilities of the second generation leaders have been valued and whether they have been treated as equal participants in the leadership process. In addition, Issues #4 and #6 will provide indirect information on the participants' sense of valuation. If the participants' responses to the survey regarding these five issues appear to be consistent with retention, then these issues collectively provide evidence to argue that "sense of valuation" has a relationship to retention.

CHAPTER 2

LITERATURE REVIEW

This project takes seriously the vital role of effective spiritual leadership development in the health and growth of second-generation Vietnamese within the local church. In Jesus' early ministry right after his baptism, he called disciples to follow him as he travelled from city to city to heal the sick and to preach about the coming of the kingdom of God. In Jesus' strategy for making disciples, he allowed his disciples witness how he ministered to others; in fact, Jesus went through many towns and villages, teaching in their synagogues, preaching the good news of the kingdom, and healing every disease and sickness (Matt 9:35).

The importance of leadership development and discipleship is further emphasized by the Apostle Paul who instructs the leaders of the church in Ephesians to focus on equipping God's people for doing

God's work and building up the church as one body of Christ (Eph. 4:12). In other words, the concept of training the church's spiritual leaders and equipping them for the work of God is an important component in the life of the church, and that is why there are many books, articles, and conferences that focus on identifying the factors that contribute to the annual decline in church attendance. Unfortunately, even though a majority of the Asian immigrant churches today in America are experiencing an exodus of the second generation, the first-generation Vietnamese pastors have failed to identify the factors that are causing many younger people to leave their heritage churches. Failure to develop leadership training programs for the second generation due to a lack of vision and lack of resources has become a common issue in many immigrant churches nationwide; this phenomenon is happening in mainstream American churches as well.

A purposeful method of developing potential leaders within the second generation of Vietnamese in a local church is not the only factor necessary to promote church health and growth. However, it is an important factor because the next generation of spiritual leaders needs to lead others in order for the church to continue to go and make disciples according the Great Commission (Matt. 28: 18-20). The exodus of the second-generation of Vietnamese from their heritage churches in America today reflects that the existing fellowship of the first-generation Vietnamese pastors nationwide does not have a long-term vision for engaging the second generation of Vietnamese in church ministry and leadership. In fact, the first-generation Vietnamese pastors have not developed the necessary tools to equip others effectively. Because the first-generation pastors do not embrace a biblical mandate or vision for discipling the younger generation or for updating their traditional church structure and worship styles, they look at potential leaders among the second generation of Vietnamese as a threat to their vocations within church. Consequently, the fulfillment of the Great Commission is hindered.

In *Leaders on Leadership,* George Barna states that even the mainstream American church today is experiencing declining participation due to a lack of strong leadership.[79] As a result, the decline of the younger generation today in both American churches and immigrant churches is due to cultural differences between the two generations, as well as differences in their worldviews. Furthermore, in the instance of the Vietnamese immigrant churches, a majority of the first-generation Vietnamese pastors only look at the fulfilling the Great Commission through the small lens of making disciples through biblical teaching, rather than through lifestyle modeling. In other words, when a training session is offered to train church members how to make disciples within

---

[79] George Barna, *Leaders on Leadership* (Ventura: Regal, 1997), 18.

the Vietnamese church in the United States, every attendee believes that he or she will instantly become a teacher and trainer to train others as disciple makers. Thus, attendees come to a training class for making disciples believing that they will then be able to go and teach others how to make disciples, but this is not the way that Jesus prepared his disciples. In addition to teaching biblical principles, Jesus demonstrated those biblical principles in action and modeled godly leadership qualities to his own disciples before he ascended.

An intentional strategy for developing and engaging potential leaders from the second generation of Vietnamese and for yielding a higher rate of second-generation retention in the local church will take seriously both the practical experience of the process of leadership development and the instruction on the biblical mandate of discipleship. The presence of intergenerational differences within the Vietnamese church in the United States is unavoidable, and these cultural differences represent the Vietnamese/Asian cultural values versus American/Western cultural values of the first and second generation Vietnamese respectively. It is necessary to recognize the cultural differences and their nuances which directly or indirectly affect the "silent exodus" of the second generation of Vietnamese in order to improve the rate of retention of the second generation in the church.[80]

In view of the issues confronting Vietnamese immigrant churches as outlined in Chapter 1, the following literature review focuses more broadly on factors that contribute to the decreasing involvement of younger people in immigrant American churches as well as in mainstream American churches. The factors presented here provide the foundation for the research tool developed by the current researcher in his exploration of reasons for declining retention of the younger generation in Vietnamese churches.

WORK THAT ADDRESSES HEALTHY VIETNAMESE-AMERICAN CHURCH LIFE AND THE RETENTION OF THE VIETNAMESE YOUNGER GENERATION

Very little research has focused specifically on the Vietnamese church in America. Thuan Nguyen's 2014 dissertation for Alliance Theological Seminary establishes rigorously, as has been outlined in Chapter 1, that first-generation Vietnamese pastors are high power distance and second generation Vietnamese church leaders are low power-distance, to use Hofstede's language. While Nguyen suggests that this cultural difference in the concept of authority contributes to

---

[80] Helen Lee. "Silent Exodus – Can the East Asian Church in America Reverse the Flight of its Next Generation," n.p. *Christianity Today* (Dec 1996). Cited 29 August 2013. Online: http://www.ctlibrary.com/ct/1996/august12/6t9050.html.

communication problems, he does not prove that there is a connection between this difference and the retention of the second generation. This connection will be one of the focuses of the present study.[81]

WORKS THAT ADDRESS HEALTHY CHURCH LIFE FOR KOREAN-AMERICAN AND OTHER ASIAN-AMERICAN CHURCHES

In *Growing Healthy Asian American Churches,* edited by Peter Cha, S. Steve Kang, and Helen Lee, the writers claim that one hindrance to a healthy Asian American church is when the leader shapes the model of his leadership based solely on his own culture, instead of on Christ's culture.[82] The work of this present researcher is examining whether this hindrance does, in fact, affect retention of young people within Vietnamese immigrant churches in America today. In the discussions presented in this book, the editors believe that it is time for the first generation of pastors and leaders to learn to value team ministry instead of performing their duties solely through their own personal strength and sacrifice.[83] In total, the authors present four particularly important skills for today's leaders of healthy Asian American

---

[81] Q4 and Q5 on the SGVFG Survey touch upon some aspects of the power distance between generations.

[82] Peter Cha, Steve Kang and Helen Lee, eds., *Growing Healthy Asian American Churches: Ministry Insights from Groundbreaking Congregations* (Downers Grove, IL: InterVarsity Press, 2006), 60.

[83] Ibid., 93.

churches. In addition to learning to value team ministry, pastors need to pursue a balanced life, demonstrate vulnerability, and recognize God's leadership.[84] The present study investigates specifically the relationship between the valuation of team ministry and the retention of the younger generation.

A similar scenario is also happening among immigrant families who came from India, according to Ashish Raichur, in his article *The Second Generation: Spiritual and Cultural Conflict*. Raichur astutely addresses the same problem within the Indian churches in America, which is that church leaders have failed to provide for the spiritual needs of the second generation, resulting in a major gap between the two generations; thus, the younger generation typically does not like to attend their parents' churches. Like many immigrant churches, the Indian church often becomes a gathering location for social forums and cultural activities for those in the first generation to live in their past.[85]

Another goal of the present researcher is to evaluate the retention of the younger people based on the discussion in *Worship on the Way: Exploring Asian North American Christian Experience* written by Russell Yee, in which the author claims that cultural differences within

---

[84] Peter Cha, Steve Kang and Helen Lee, 93.

[85] Ashish Raichur, "The Second Generation: Spiritual and Cultural Conflicts," n.p. *Agape Partners International*. Cited on 5th November 2014. Online: http://agapepartners.org/articles/34/1/The-Second-GenerationSpiritual-and-Cultural-Conflicts/Page1.html.

a church will be a challenging factor in the retention of the young people. Yee believes that worship represents the cultures of those who are gathered to worship; thus, using the differences in cultures as a God-given palette is a key point in resolving the retention matter because God is pleased with corporate offerings of worship which blend the characteristics of the participants.[86] In other words, church pastors and leaders can stimulate the retention of their young people in a church where two different generational cultures exist by cultivating and sharing a common commitment and vision for the church.[87] Although Yee's observation is significant, the present study will not investigate specifically whether worship style played a role in retention—only the opportunities to serve in the worship service.

The bottom line for yielding a high rate of retention of the second generation is to maintain verbal communication between the first and the second generation of Vietnamese within a church; a healthy mandate for personal discipleship and communication will likely positively affect retention of young people. In other words, when cultural differences are addressed and resolved through open communication, God's

---

[86] Russell Yee, *Worship on the Way: Exploring Asian North American Christian Experience* (Valley Forge, PA: Judson Press, 2012), 68.

[87] Peter Cha, Steve Kang and Helen Lee, eds., *Growing Healthy Asian American Churches: Ministry Insights from Groundbreaking Congregations* (Downers Grove, IL: InterVarsity Press, 2006), 90.

glory can be realized, and perhaps conflict can be minimized, which will likely result in increased retention of young people.

Another related element presented by Eunice Or, *Understanding and Mentorship to Support Second Generation Church Leaders*, is that when the first generation leaders take initiative to show concern and humility toward the younger people, these observable actions may encourage the second generation to desire to serve God and stay involved in the church.[88] In this research study, Or's claim will be tested to seek whether its implementation contributes to the retention of the younger people in Vietnamese church.[89]

In regard to narrowing the gap between the first and the second generations, Russell Yee cites the importance of unity through the example of Ken Kong, a Cambodian American, who started the "New Urban Voice," which calls both the first and the second generations to come together to serve the Lord. Yee and Kong believe that unity can be achieved through the first generation asking forgiveness from the second generations and releasing them to serve by blessing, welcoming, and treating the second generation of Christians as full partners.[90] This

---

[88] Eunice Or, "Understanding and Mentorship to Support Second Generation Church Leaders," n.p. Cited 25 February 2015. Online: http://l2foundation.org/2007/supporting-second-generation-church-leaders.

[89] Q5 on the SGVFG survey asks participants if they believe(d) the church leaders made it easy for them to talk about their spiritual needs.

[90] Russell Yee, *Worship on the Way: Exploring Asian North American Christian Experience* (Valley Forge, PA: Judson Press, 2012), 126.

present researcher is testing whether this type of positive action and attitude from first generation pastors affects retention of the second generation of Vietnamese in America.[91]

In "Galatians and Korean Immigrants," a study of generational conflict in Korean immigration churches, Sejong Chun claims that another hindrance to the retention of the younger people is a "lack of ideological vision" for harmonious unity in Christ. This is because the second generation of Koreans considers themselves Americans, instead of living in a so-called "mono-racial" and "mono-cultural" society under their parents.[92] The researcher is testing whether this hindrance also affects retention of young people.

However, another study, written by Pyong Gap Min relating to Asian Americans, more specifically to the second generation of the Korean church in New York City, also offers insight into the retention of the type of young people that the present researcher is examining. The author's interviews with the second generation of Koreans reveal that second-generation Korean Protestants show a higher rate of retention in their childhood religion than their counterparts from other Asian immigrant groups. Surprisingly, second generation Korean Christians

---

[91] Q5 on the SGVFG survey asks participants if they were treated by church leaders as their equals.

[92] Sejong Chun, "Galatians and Korean Immigrants," n.p. Cited 25 February 2015. Online: http://www.vanderbilt.edu/AnS/religious_studies/GBC/sejongchun.doc.

tend not to celebrate their Korean traditional or national holidays.[93] In addition, in their congregational services, second generation Koreans seldom make reference to the Korean community in their sermons. Furthermore, second generation Koreans do not believe that churches should play any role in preserving Korean culture.[94] Rather, their priority is that the church should focus on spreading the gospel rather than on retaining Korean culture.[95]

In a separate publication, *Preserving Ethnicity through Religion in America: Korean Protestants and Indian Hindus Across Generations*, Pyong Gap Min further highlights the importance of the decision of the Korean church to minimize the focus on preservation of culture to the detriment of biblical priorities. Min shows that when first- generation Korean churches consider their church a place to preserve Korean language and Korean Confucian customs and values, those churches fail to retain their young people.[96] The Korean and Indian churches that Min presents in this study have the potential for generational parallels to the "silent exodus" that the Vietnamese church is experiencing. In the absence of academic studies related directly to the Vietnamese church,

---

[93] Pyong Gap Min, ed., *Asian American: Contemporary Trends and Issues* (Thousand Oaks, California: Pine Forge Press, 2006), 254.

[94] Ibid., 254.

[95] Ibid., 254.

[96] Pyong Gap Min, *Preserving Ethnicity through Religion in America: Korean Protestants and Indian Hindus Across Generations* (New York, NY: New York University Press, 2010), 198.

Vietnamese pastors and leaders should consider reviewing the evidence from such studies and learning from the successes and failures of other Asian churches and applying the principles that can be learned to their own churches.[97]

In another study, *Intergenerational Transmission of Religion and Culture: Korean Protestants in the U.S.*, Pyong Gap Min and Dae Young Kim argue that transmitting a religion from the immigrant parents to the second generation of Koreans born in the United States does not necessarily help to transmit ethnic culture and ethnic identity unless there is a strong correlation between the two. In this article, the authors challenge the practice of having two different worship services for the first and the second generation; they feel that gathering together for worship in the same place is essential, especially when religion is being transmitted from the immigrant parents.[98] Even though the authors' suggestion supports an alternative way for the two generations of Koreans to maintain their healthy church and has intuitive merit, its application may not be an important element for other minority churches like Vietnamese immigrant churches to implement.

---

[97] Q6 on the SGVFG survey asks participants if they can /could relate to the Vietnamese Church's vision of reaching Vietnamese for Christ.

[98] Pyong Gap Min and Dae Young Kim, Intergenerational Transmission of Religion and Culture: Korean Protestants in the U.S. *Sociology of Religion, A Quarterly Review*, Vol. 66, Issue 3, pp. 263-282. Cited 25 February 2015. Online: http://socrel.oxfordjournals.org/content/66/3/263.abstract.

In another branch of the discussion in regard to retention of the younger immigrant generations in ethnic churches, the authors Carolyn Chen and Russell Jeung, in *Sustaining Faith Traditions: Race, Ethnicity, and Religion among the Latino and Asian American Second Generation*, have made two significant claims. The first is that immigrant churches will be faced with their aging sooner or later; thus, in order to survive, the first-generation church should seek to transition to a more inclusive multiethnic congregational model, with less emphasis on maintaining the heritage culture. Second, when there is a sizable first-generation as well as a growing second-generation, the two generations might choose to worship in the same building, but independently, with separate worship services—one service in the mother tongue for their first generation and the other in English for the growing generations.[99] This researcher will explore whether implementation of the use of the English language might affect the retention of the second generation of Vietnamese in America today.

In Soulit Chacko's thesis, *Treading Identities*, he quotes from Pyong Gap Min's argument to describe how second-generation Korean Americans stress their religious identity as their primary identity and their ethnic identity as their secondary identity over the American

---

[99] Carolyn Chen and Russell Jeung, *In Sustaining Faith Traditions: Race, Ethnicity, and Religion among the Latino and Asian American Second Generation* (New York, NY: New York University Press, 2012), 177-178.

identity,[100] but he does not compare the differences in religious and ethnic identities between the first and the second generation of Korean Christians. In fact, these differences are one of the issues addressed in the present researcher's project.[101]

Another possible contributing factor to the present study of the researcher regarding the retention of young people is found in Joan Huyser-Honig's article, in which she discusses the ideal of engaging younger people in learning and participating in the church's worship. In her article outlining a design for intergenerational worship, she claims that at least one positive element that could assist in the growth of the worship service is for leaders to look for ways to address the needs of different ages in different parts of the service and not to assume that only adults of a certain age really care about worship.[102] This article describes a healthy worship service with intergenerational worship; however, the author of the article does not discuss this element as a solution for the younger generation's retention. The present study will

---

[100] Soulit Chacko, "Treading Identities: Second-Generation Christian Indian Americans Negotiating Race, Ethnicity and Religion in America," n.p. Cited 26 February 2015. Online: http://ecommons.luc.edu/cgi/viewcontent.cgi?article=2852&context=luc_theses.

[101] Q6 on the SGVFG Survey asks about whether the participant's vision of outreach was narrowed to reaching the Vietnamese.

[102] Joan Huyser-Honig, "Nine Tips for Designing Intergenerational Worship," n.p. Cited 25 February 2015. Online: http://worship.calvin.edu/resources/resource-library/nine-tips-for-designing-intergenerational-worship/

explore whether this factor relates to the younger generation's retention in Vietnamese churches.[103]

In another discussion related to the matter of the first and second generation of Koreans, the author Sharon Kim clearly identifies at least two obstacles that contribute to the exodus from church of the second generation of Koreans who were born or raised in America. First, the younger potential leaders were often treated as merely workers at the very bottom of the chain of command, which made them felt uncomfortable and oppressed. Secondly, church leaders were overly hierarchical and dictatorial instead of seeing the young people as their equals in service to the Lord, which led to the failure to retain the second generation within Korean churches.[104] These two possible obstacles directly contribute to the present focus of the researcher's study.[105]

In *Seeking a New Spiritual Home: The Study of Chinese Christian Churches and Communities in the United States*, Yi-Chya Ting addresses the cultural conflict between the first and the second generations of Chinese Christians. The author proposes that one of the obvious obstacles that Chinese churches often face is different concepts of church priorities between the first and second generation cultures,

---

[103] Q1 asks about second generation participation in Sunday worship.

[104] Sharon Kim, *A Faith of Our Own: Second-Generation Spirituality in Korean American Churches* (Piscataway, NJ: Rutgers University Press, 2010), 1.

[105] Q5 in the survey asks about being treated as equals.

where the first generation is strict in observing traditions and rituals, stressing hierarchy and authority. This is completely in opposition to the second generation which concentrates more on Christian ethics and sharing the gospel.[106] While Yi-Chya Ting suggests that the differing cultural concepts and priorities cause conflict within a Chinese church, he does not prove that there is a connection between this conflict and the retention of the second generation. As the matter of fact, even though the present study does not specifically include questions about Vietnamese concepts of hierarchy and authority, the study does address the lack of shared leadership, which is connected to these concepts.[107]

Finally, another discovery connected to the present study regarding the church's retention of the second generation, comes from Peter Ong in his article *Exist Wounds*, where he argues that the second generation of immigrants tend to look for a church where they can engage with people in expressing their thoughts and emotions as well as discovering their voice among others.[108] Peter Ong perfectly describes a connec-

---

[106] Yi-Chya Ting, *Seeking a New Spiritual Home: The Study of Chinese Christian Churches and Communities in the United States*. http://search.proquest.com/docview/304941660. (Accessed: Feb. 25th, 2015).

[107] Q5 in the survey asks about being treated as equals.

[108] Peter Ong, "Exist Wounds: The Flight of Asian American Faith," n.p. Cited 25 February 2015. Online: https://peterong.wordpress.com/2006/10/20/exit-wounds-the-flight-of-asian-american-faith-published/.

tion between this priority of the young people and the possibility for retention of the second generation.[109]

WORKS THAT ADDRESS AMERICAN CHURCH LIFE AND THE RETENTION OF THE YOUNGER GENERATION

In *After the Baby Boomers: How Twenty- and Thirty-Somethings Are Shaping the Future of American Religion*, Princeton sociologist Robert Wuthnow examines the relationship between religion and society with regard to the young adults in America today who were born after the baby boomer generation. The author cites another potential hindrance to the retention of the younger generation in the church; he believes that unless religious leaders take younger adults more seriously, the future of American religion is in doubt.[110] Even though Robert Wuthnow's research focuses on the retention of young people in American mainstream churches, the same principle may apply to ethnic immigrant churches. The present researcher will seek to determine whether the issue of how much the first generation respects the

---

[109] Q4 in the survey asks about whether the church leaders made it easy for their young people to talk about their spiritual needs.

[110] Robert Wuthnow, *After the Baby Boomers: How Twenty-and Thirty-Somethings Are Shaping the Future of American Religion* (Princeton, NJ: Princeton University Press, 2007), 17.

second generation is a factor in the retention of the second generation of Vietnamese today.[111]

Another aspect of retention that the current research will examine is presented by Joseph M. Stowell, the author of *Shepherding the Church: Effective Spiritual Leadership in a Changing Culture*, who believes that effective leadership in a changing culture demands church leaders to maintain the dynamic love of Christ, a model of "leading through loving," which will establish an effective spiritual foundation.[112] In other words, developing an attitude of Christ-likeness will help church leaders to focus on loving the members and will have the added benefit of building the kingdom culture of Christ instead of the kingdom culture of man. In addition, even though *Developing Your Next Generation of Church Leaders* written by Steven Saccone and Cheri Saccone does not directly address a solution for a higher rate of second generation retention within the Vietnamese churches, the priority of having the mature generations of pastors focus more intentionally on furthering the kingdom of God by nurturing the younger generations is relevant to the present project.[113]

---

[111] Q5 in the survey asks about being treated as equals.

[112] Joseph M. Stowell, *Shepherding the Church: Effective Spiritual Leadership in a Changing Culture* (Chicago: Moody Press, 1997), 177-178.

[113] Steve Saccone and Cheri Saccone, *Developing Your Next Generation of Church Leaders* (Downers Grove, Illinois: IVP Books, 2012), 22-23.

Today's discussion regarding the retention of younger people in the church is not an issue only within the immigrant churches in the U.S. In fact, American Anglo churches are also seeking effective methods for the retention of their young people. In Shellnutt's argument, she advocates that church leaders should connect their church activities to social media sites since young people who were born in the '80s and '90s have grown up as digital natives.[114] Her claims are supported by the high percentages of young people who use Twitter, Facebook, and Instagram. Shellnutt presents many insights for retaining the second generation using digital means which may also be applicable to Vietnamese church situation.

In *Are Millennials Really Leaving the Church?* Bob Smietana cites two hindrances to the church's retention of young people as proposed by Sánchez-Walsh. Sánchez-Walsh states that the church should change to reflect the diversity of today's American society. An additional hindrance to the retention of the younger people identified by Sánchez-Walsh is that current church leaders from the older generation are reluctant to give up their power. However, she observes that demographic shifts are going to force churches and the current people

---

[114] Kate Shellnutt, "33 Under 33: Meet the Christian leaders shaping the next generation of our faith," n.p. Cited 25 February 2015. Online: http://www.christianitytoday.com/ct/2014/july-august/33-under-33.html.

in power to confront this issue of unwillingness to relinquish control.[115] Even though the above discussion pertains primarily to white millennials, this present researcher is testing whether this hindrance affects retention of young people within the Vietnamese churches.[116]

R. Channing Johnson, in *Where Have All the Young People Gone*, reminds his reader to look at the church and compare it to a family. The church today should play the role of family where beliefs and values are stable, and it should also serve as a social security system, where healthy children will be a true blessing to aging parents who can be cared for in their later years as part of that big family.[117] Johnson is concerned that many church pastors and leaders have forgotten that even though people are different, they still want to be treated as a valuable part of the family of Christ.

There are at least four major issues that Johnson articulates as reasons that young people have left their churches. The first reason is that church people are often judgmental in trying to show that they are right and others are wrong. The second reason is that church people are

---

[115] Bob Smietana, "*Are Millennials Really Leaving the Church? Yes-but mostly White millennials*," n.p. Cited 25 February 2015. Online: http://www.faithstreet.com/onfaith/2014/05/16/are-millennials-really-leaving-church-yes-but-mostly-white-millennials/32103.

[116] Q1, Q3, Q5 and Q7 on the SGVFG survey all pertain to some aspect of shared leadership in the Vietnamee Church.

[117] R. Channing Johnson, *Where Have All the Young People Gone: Exploring Generational Change and How young People Can be Reached* (Glendale, Arizona: USA, 2012), 1-2.

perceived as being hypocritical and as acting like they have the right to judge everybody else, yet neglect to admit their own shortcomings. The third reason is that church people commonly respond negatively to homosexuals if they discover a gay relationship within the church membership. The fourth reason is that church people are described as intolerant and try to impose their beliefs on others.[118]

Even though Johnson's proposed reasons that young people have left their churches are derived predominantly from studies of Caucasian American churches, the same issues likely exist within the Vietnamese immigrant churches today in America. In other words, since the second-generation Vietnamese are raised in America as members of a young post-modern generation, they are likely to follow the practices of their peers in seeking ideas and values that are worthwhile to incorporate into their own worldviews, and they frequently want to have knowledge of religions other than Christianity.[119] As a result, many second-generation Vietnamese choose not to return to their heritage churches or decide to transfer to American churches because they have grown up with negative experiences with Vietnamese churches and pastors who had a tradition of rejecting and criticizing all lifestyles that did not fit their traditional images of a Christian lifestyle.

---

[118] R. Channing Johnson, 105-106.

[119] Ibid., 107.

CHAPTER 3

METHODOLOGY

The goal of this research project is to identify factors that may contribute to a higher retention rate of the younger Vietnamese generation in Vietnamese immigrant churches. Each aspect of the research will be described in detail below, but in brief, this project focuses on Vietnamese and Montagnard (Vietnamese tribal groups) Christian immigrant churches and invites participants from the second generation to respond to a Likert Scale survey designed by the researcher. The results of the survey were tabulated to determine which of the elements included in the survey contributed to a higher retention rate among the younger Vietnamese generation through the responses of randomly selected survey participants from Vietnamese and Montagnard churches.

PARTICIPANTS

As participants in the project, three different groups were included. The first group (Group A) consisted of members of the younger Vietnamese generations who were still attending Vietnamese churches. The second group (Group B) contained individuals from the younger Vietnamese generations who had attended a Vietnamese Church for at least two years in the past, but are now attending non-Vietnamese churches. The third group (Group C) was comprised of members of the younger Vietnamese generations who had previously attended a Vietnamese Church for at least two years, but have not attended any church since they left their Vietnamese heritage churches.

In other words, Group A represents younger Vietnamese who have been "retained" in the Vietnamese Church, and Groups B and C represent younger Vietnamese who have not been "retained." The participants ranged in age from sixteen to thirty-three years old. In order to participate in this survey, the young people had to have been members of Vietnamese churches or Montagnard churches for at least two years. The two year requirement applied to all three of the groups described above. This survey included participants who are currently involved or had been previously involved in Vietnamese and Montagnard churches under the Christian and Missionary Alliance on the east coast.

The participants in this project who are still attending the Vietnamese church (Group A) are living in Raleigh, North Carolina, and the other participants, who are attending non-Vietnamese churches or not attending church at all, are geographically located throughout the United States. The researcher's relationship with these participants in all three categories comes from many years of friendship as a youth leader serving among them since 1998 around the country. The diversity of the participants provided a rich perspective of responses regarding their spiritual needs as well as their love of participating in ministry to serve others.

The following is an abbreviated summary of the demographics of the participants whose surveys were randomly chosen to be tabulated as the results of the study. (The complete information can be found in Appendices C, D, and E.) The participants in Group A, the retained group, are those who have remained involved in the Vietnamese or Montagnard churches of the Christian and Missionary Alliance in the Raleigh, North Carolina, area. Twenty-nine of the participants were from the Vietnamese church, and 21 were from the Montagnard church. The age of the participants in this group ranged from 16 to 29, with the average age of 21.4 years of age. The length of time that these young people had been involved in their respective churches ranged from 5 years to 19 years, and the average length of involvement was 10.62 years.

The groups that were not retained, Group B and Group C, were demographically similar to Group A in many ways. In Group B, the group which remained involved in church but are no longer involved in their heritage churches, had an average age of 23.14, and their ages ranged from 19 to 29 years old. The number of years that they had been involved in Vietnamese churches ranged from 2 to 9 years for an average of 5.72 years. The surveys indicated that young people in this group are now attending churches of many different denominations, including Baptist, Lutheran, Presbyterian, Assemblies of God, Calvary Chapel, and Methodist. (See Appendix C, D, E for a detailed list and the distribution between the various types of churches.) For Group C, the group of young people who are no longer attending church, the age of the participants ranged from 19 to 29, with the average age being 23.14. The length of time that they had spent in the Vietnamese church varied from 2 years to 9 years, with 5.5 years as the average length of time. Interestingly, even though the minimum time of involvement required for participation in the study was 2 years, the majority of the participants had spent much more time in the Vietnamese church; in fact, the average was over 5 years for both Group B and Group C. These non-retained young people had thoroughly experienced life in the Vietnamese church; thus, it cannot be said that they rejected the Vietnamese church without really being involved in it.

DATA COLLECTION

From September 2014 through January 2015, 150 potential participants from each of the 3 previously-described groups were invited to participate voluntarily in the study and were provided with a copy of the survey instrument, consisting of the "Second Generation Valuation by First Generation Scale" (SGVFG Scale). (A copy of the SGVFG Scale is available in Appendix A) Group A consisted of 150 young people who are still attending either the Vietnamese or Montagnard Alliance churches in the Raleigh area; both the Vietnamese church and the Montagnard church in North Carolina are under the South Atlantic District of the Christian and Missionary Alliance. Participants of this group were invited to participate in this research in person on Sunday, November 30, 2014, from 3:00pm – 4:00pm during the weekend of the Thanksgiving week. An introductory presentation was given to help participants understand the purpose of this project, which was to discern the factors that result in retention of the younger Vietnamese generation within the Vietnamese church and the Montagnard church. The researcher randomly selected only 50 out of the 150 responses that came from Group A.

The other two groups, those who are attending non-Vietnamese churches (Group B) and those who are no longer attending any church (Group C), were invited to participate in this research project through e-mail. The invitations were extended electronically via e-mails, and a letter was attached to the e-mail explaining the purpose of this research, which was to help the researcher discover the factors that result in retention of the younger Vietnamese generation in their heritage churches (A copy of the invitation letter is available in Appendix B). All who participated did so voluntarily through personal invitation of the researcher, and they were all guaranteed complete anonymity in their participation. The surveys were sent out electronically via email by the researcher, and over 100 responses from both Group B and Group C were received via e-mail. The researcher randomly chose only 50 out of the more than 100 responses that came from each of these groups.

DATA COLLECTION INSTRUMENT

The Second Generation Valuation by First Generation Scale

(SGVFG Scale – See Appendix A)

The survey consisting of the SGVFG Scale contained fourteen questions.[120] The age to participate in the survey was limited to sixteen to twenty-six years of age. The first group of participants (Group

---

[120] See Appendix A.

A) consisted of those still attending the Vietnamese and Montagnard churches in Raleigh under the South Atlantic District of the Christian and Missionary Alliance. The participants in the other two groups, those who attend non-Vietnamese churches (Group B) and those who never attend church (Group C), formerly attended either Vietnamese Alliance churches under the Vietnamese District of the C&MA or Vietnamese Baptist churches. The general focus of the fourteen questions in the survey was to discuss the factors that motivate the younger generation of Vietnamese to stay and to be involved in their heritage churches.

The questions were structured for response in the Likert Scale format, which is effective in evaluating how much the younger generation felt valued by the Vietnamese church leadership. The Likert Scale formulated for this research asks for the level of agreement each participant felt with respect to statements designed to reveal attitudes about his or her experience while attending a Vietnamese church. The design of the scale provides for a range of responses that can be categorized in the areas of agreement or disagreement. The researcher used these survey questions to gain information about the Vietnamese leadership style in the following areas:

1. Importance of worship service integration of the second generation of Vietnamese. (Q1)

2. Knowledge and recognition of potential leaders among the second generation of Vietnamese. (Q2 and Q3)

3. Importance of exhibiting a certain level of respect for the leadership ability of others. (Q3)

4. Knowledge and understanding of the spiritual walk of the second generation of Vietnamese. (Q4)

5. Understanding of leadership's relationship to other co-workers. (Q5)

6. Ability to transmit ministry vision to others. (Q6)

7. Importance of cross-cultural adaptation within one's church. (Q7)

CHAPTER 4

FINDINGS

The desired outcome of this research project is to identify factors that may potentially enhance the retention rate of the younger Vietnamese generation in the Vietnamese churches nationwide. The purpose of this study is to discover the relationship between retention and the successful integration of potential leaders from the younger generation of Vietnamese into church leadership. Engaging the younger Vietnamese generations in leadership is a necessary component of making disciples within the immigrant Vietnamese community.

The results of this project will hopefully help to equip and empower the first generation of Vietnamese leaders and pastors in discerning the importance of lovingly nurturing the second generation and preparing them for the ministry God has given to all generations.

SURVEY RESULTS

The analysis of the survey data will be presented in the same numerical order as the questions in the survey. The first five questions address leadership awareness, and the last two questions address the church environment. The average score for each group will be reported for each question, and this score will reflect whether the participants generally responded with *strongly agree (SA), agree (A), neutral (N), disagree (DA), or strongly disagree (DS).*

Issue #1 (Q1 and Q1A): Performing Tasks for the Sunday Worship Service

For Question 1, the Group A responses indicate that fifty-six percent *strongly agreed* that during periods of regularly attending a Vietnamese church, they were actively performing tasks on a regular basis for the Sunday worship service, whereas thirty percent *agreed* that they were actively performing tasks on a regular basis for the Sunday service, fourteen percent were *neutral*, no one selected *disagreed*, and no one selected *strongly disagree* as the response. The average score that Group A selected, based on SA=5, A=4, N=3, D=2, SD=1, is 4.42.

For Group B, Question 1 responses indicate that forty-two percent *strongly agreed* that they were actively performing tasks on a regular basis for the Sunday worship service, whereas fifty-eight percent *agreed* that they were actively performing tasks regularly for the Sunday worship service. In this group, no one selected *neutral, disagree*, or *strongly disagree* for this question. The average score that Group B selected, based on SA=5, A=4, N=3, D=2, SD=1, is 4.42.

For Group C, Question 1, the responses indicate that fifty-eight percent *strongly agreed* that they were actively performing tasks on a regular basis for the Sunday worship service, and an additional forty percent *agreed* that they were actively performing tasks on a regular basis for the Sunday worship service. Two percent were *neutral*, no one selected *disagree*, and no one selected *strongly disagree* as the answer. The average score that Group C selected, based on SA=5, A=4, N=3, D=2, SD=1, is 4.56.

In the additional Question 1A, for Group A, the responses indicate that thirty percent *strongly agreed* that it is important to them that they are actively performing tasks on a regular basis for the Sunday worship service, and forty-six percent *agreed* that it is important to them that they are actively performing tasks on a regular basis for the Sunday worship service; twenty-four were *neutral*, no one selected *disagree*, and no one selected *strongly disagree* as the answer. The average score that Group A selected, based on SA=5, A=4, N=3, D=2, SD=1, is 4.06.

For Group B, Question 1A, the responses indicate that sixty-four percent *strongly agreed* that it is important for them to perform tasks on a regular basis for the Sunday worship service, whereas thirty percent *agreed* that it is important for them to perform tasks on a regular basis for the Sunday worship service, six percent were *neutral*, no one selected *disagree*, and no one selected *strongly disagree* as the answer. The average score that Group B selected, based on SA=5, A=4, N=3, D=2, SD=1, is 4.58.

For Group C, Question 1A, the responses indicate that six percent *strongly agreed* that it is important for them to perform tasks on a regular basis for the Sunday worship service, whereas forty-four percent *agreed* that it is important for them to perform tasks on a regular basis for the Sunday worship service, fifty percent were *neutral*, no one selected *disagree*, and no one selected *strongly disagree* as the answer. The average score that Group C selected, based on SA=5, A=4, N=3, D=2, SD=1, is 3.56.

The following is a comparison chart providing a summary of the responses regarding Issue #1(Q1 and Q1A): Performing Tasks for the Sunday Worship Service.

Chart #1: Performing Tasks for the Sunday Worship Service.

Question	Group A	Group B	Group C
1	4.42	4.42	4.56
1A	4.06	4.58	3.56

Issue #2 (Q2 and Q2A): Valuation of Active Involvement from the Older Generation

On Question 2, for Group A, the responses indicate that sixty percent *strongly agreed* that during periods of regularly attending a Vietnamese church, they believed that the older Vietnamese congregants valued their active involvement in church events, whereas thirty-eight percent *agreed* that they believed that the older Vietnamese congregants valued their younger generation's active involvement in church event. Two percent were *neutral*, no one selected *disagree*, and no one selected *strongly disagree* as the answer. The average score that Group A selected, based on SA=5, A=4, N=3, D=2, SD=1, is 4.58.

For Group B, Question 2, the responses indicate that seventy-four percent *strongly disagreed* that the older Vietnamese valued their active involvement in church events; another twenty-two percent *disagreed* that during periods of regularly attending a Vietnamese church the older Vietnamese valued their active involvement in church events. Four percent were *neutral* on whether the older Vietnamese valued their active involvement in church events, no one selected *agree*, and no one selected *strongly agree* as the answer. The average score that Group B selected, based on SA=5, A=4, N=3, D=2, SD=1, is 1.3.

For Group C, Question 2, the responses indicate that sixty-two percent *strongly disagreed* that during periods of regularly attending a Vietnamese church, the older Vietnamese congregants valued their active involvement in church events, and an additional thirty-eight percent *disagreed* that the older Vietnamese congregants valued their active involvement in church events. No one selected *neutral*, no one selected *agree*, and no one selected *strongly agree* as the answer. The average score that Group C selected, based on SA=5, A=4, N=3, D=2, SD=1, is 1.38.

On the additional Question 2A, for Group A, the responses indicated that sixty-four percent *strongly agreed* that it is important to them that the older generation values their active involvement in church events, whereas thirty-six percent *agreed* that it is important to them that the older Vietnamese should value their active involvement in church events, two percent were *neutral*, no one selected *disagree*, and no one selected *strongly disagree* as the answer. The average score that Group A selected, based on SA=5, A=4, N=3, D=2, SD=1, is 4.64.

For Group B, Question 2A, the responses indicate that thirty percent *strongly agreed* that it is important to them that the older generation values their active involvement in church events, whereas sixty-eight percent *agreed* that it is important to them, two percent selected *neutral*, no one selected *disagree*, and no one selected *strongly disagree* as the answer. The average score that Group B selected, based on SA=5, A=4, N=3, D=2, SD=1, is 4.28.

For Group C, Question 2A, the responses indicate that thirty-six percent *strongly agreed* that it is important to them that the older generation values their active involvement in church events, whereas sixty-four percent *agreed* that it is important to them that the older Vietnamese value their active involvement in church events. No other answers were selected for this question. The average score that Group C selected, based on SA=5, A=4, N=3, D=2, SD=1, is 4.36.

The following chart provides a comparison summary for Issue #2 (Q2 and Q2A): Valuation of Active Involvement from the Older Generation.

Chart #2: Active Involvement in Church Valued by Older Vietnamese

Question	Group A	Group B	Group C
2	4.58	1.3	1.38
2A	4.64	4.28	4.36

Issue #3 (Q3 and Q3A): Leadership Abilities Valued by Church Leadership

On Question 3, for Group A, the responses indicate that forty-two percent *strongly agreed* that during periods of regularly attending a Vietnamese church, they believed that their leadership abilities, whether they served in leadership or not, were valued by the church leaders, whereas fifty-eight percent *agreed* that the church leaders valued their leadership ability. No other answers were selected for this question. The average score that Group A selected, based on SA=5, A=4, N=3, D=2, SD=1, is 4.42.

For Group B, Question 3, the responses indicate that sixty-eight percent *strongly disagreed* that during periods of regularly attending a Vietnamese church, they believed that their leadership abilities, whether they served in leadership or not, were valued by church leaders, whereas twenty-eight percent dis*agreed*, four percent were *neutral*, no one selected *agree*, and no one selected *strongly agree* as the answer. The average score that Group B selected, based on SA=5, A=4, N=3, D=2, SD=1, is 1.36.

For Group C, Question 3, the responses indicate that seventy-eight percent *strongly disagreed* that during periods of regularly attending a Vietnamese church, they believed that their leadership abilities, whether they served in leadership or not, were valued by church leaders, whereas twenty-two percent *disagreed*. No other answers were selected for this question. The average score that Group C selected, based on SA=5, A=4, N=3, D=2, SD=1, is 1.22.

On the additional Question 3A, for Group A, the responses indicate that six percent *strongly agreed* that it is important to them that the church leaders value their leadership ability, whereas sixty-eight percent *agreed* that it is important to them, twenty-six were *neutral*, no one selected *disagree*, and no one selected *strongly disagree* as the answer. The average score that Group A selected, based on SA=5, A=4, N=3, D=2, SD=1, is 3.8.

For Group B, Question 3A, the responses indicate that thirty-eight percent *strongly agreed* that it is important to them that the church leaders value their leadership ability, whether they served in leadership or not, whereas fifty-eight percent *agreed* that it is important to them that church leaders value their leadership abilities. Four percent were *neutral*, no one selected *disagree*, and no one selected *strongly disagree* as the answer. The average score that Group B selected, based on SA=5, A=4, N=3, D=2, SD=1, is 4.34.

For Group C, Question 3A, the responses indicate that forty percent *strongly agreed* that it is important to them that the church leaders value their leadership ability, whereas fifty-four percent *agreed* that it is important to them that church leaders value their leadership abilities. Six percent were *neutral*, no one selected *disagreed*, and no one selected *strongly disagree* as the answer. The average score that Group C selected, based on SA=5, A=4, N=3, D=2, SD=1, is 4.34.

The following is a comparison chart for Issue #3 (Q3 and Q3A): Leadership Abilities Valued by Church Leadership

Chart #3: Leadership Abilities Valued by Church Leaders.

Question	Group A	Group B	Group C
3	4.42	1.36	1.22
3A	3.8	4.34	4.34

Issue #4 (Q4, Q4A): Ease in Talking with Church Leaders about Spiritual Needs

On Question 4, for Group A, the responses indicate that fifty-six percent *strongly agreed* that church leaders made it easy for them to talk about their spiritual needs, whereas forty-four percent *agreed* that their church leaders made it easy for them to approach the leaders regarding their spiritual needs. No other answers were selected for this question. The average score that Group A selected, based on SA=5, A=4, N=3, D=2, SD=1, is 4.56.

For Group B, Question 4, the responses indicate that fifty-four percent *strongly disagreed* that church leaders made it easy for them to talk about their spiritual needs, whereas forty-six percent *disagreed* that their church leaders made it easy for them to approach in regard to their spiritual needs. No one selected *neutral*, no one selected *agree*, and no one selected *strongly agree* as the answer. The average score that Group B selected, based on SA=5, A=4, N=3, D=2, SD=1, is 1.46.

For Group C, Question 4, the responses indicate that seventy-four percent *strongly disagreed* that church leaders made it easy for the respondent to talk about their spiritual needs, whereas twenty-two percent *disagreed* that their church leaders made it easy for them to talk about their spiritual needs. Four percent were *neutral*, no one selected *disagree*, and no one selected *strongly disagree* as the answer. The average score that Group C selected, based on SA=5, A=4, N=3, D=2, SD=1, is 1.3.

On the additional Question 4A, for Group A, the responses indicate that eight-six percent *strongly agreed* that it is important to them that they can talk freely about their spiritual needs to their church leaders; an additional fourteen percent *agreed* that it is important that they can talk to church leaders freely about their spiritual needs. No one selected *neutral*, no one selected *disagree*, and no one selected *strongly disagree* as the response. The average score that Group A selected, based on SA=5, A=4, N=3, D=2, SD=1, is 4.86.

For Group B, Question 4A, the responses indicate that sixty-four percent *strongly agreed* that it is important to them that they can talk freely about their spiritual needs to the church leaders, whereas thirty-six percent *agreed* that it is important that they can talk to church leaders freely about their spiritual needs. No one selected *neutral*, no one selected *disagree*, and no one selected *strongly disagree* as the answer. The average score that Group B selected, based on SA=5, A=4, N=3, D=2, SD=1, is 4.64.

For Group C, Question 4A, the responses indicate that sixty-two percent *strongly disagreed* that it is important that they can talk freely about their spiritual needs to the church leaders, whereas thirty-eight percent *disagreed* that it is important that they can talk to church leaders freely about their spiritual needs. No other responses were selected for this question. The average score that Group C selected, based on SA=5, A=4, N=3, D=2, SD=1, is 1.38

The following comparison chart summarizes the responses regarding Issue #4 (Q4 and Q4A): Ease in Talking with Church Leaders about Spiritual Needs.

Chart #4: Ease in Talking with Church Leaders about Spiritual Needs

Question	Group A	Group B	Group C
4	4.56	1.46	1.3
4A	4.86	4.64	1.38

Issue #5 (Q5, Q5A): Treatment as Equals by Church Leaders

On Question 5, for Group A, the responses indicate that sixty-eight percent *strongly agreed* that during periods of regularly attending a Vietnamese church, they were treated by church leaders as equals, whereas twenty-eight percent *agreed* that they were treated by church leaders as equals. Four percent were *neutral*, no one selected *disagree*, and no one selected *strongly disagree* as their answer. The average score that Group A selected, based on SA=5, A=4, N=3, D=2, SD=1, is 4.64.

For Group B, Question 5, the responses indicate that eighty-four percent *strongly disagreed* that during periods of regularly attending a Vietnamese church, they were treated by church leaders as equals, whereas sixteen percent dis*agreed* that they were treated by church leaders as equals. No other answers were selected by this group. The average score that Group B selected, based on SA=5, A=4, N=3, D=2, SD=1, is 1.16.

For Group C, Question 5, the responses indicate that seventy-four percent *strongly disagreed* that during periods of regularly attending a Vietnamese church, they were treated by church leaders as equals, whereas twenty-six percent *disagreed* that they were treated by church leaders as equals. No other answers were selected by this group. The average score that Group C selected, based on SA=5, A=4, N=3, D=2, SD=1, is 1.26.

On the additional Question 5A, for Group A, the responses indicate that fifty percent *strongly agreed* that it is important to them that Vietnamese church leaders treat them as equals, and an additional fifty percent *agreed* that it is important to them that Vietnamese church leaders treat them as equals. No one selected *neutral*, no one selected *disagree*, and no one selected *strongly disagree* as their answer. The average score that Group A selected, based on SA=5, A=4, N=3, D=2, SD=1, is 4.5.

For Group B, Question 5A, the responses indicate that twenty-four percent *strongly agreed* that it is important to them that Vietnamese church leaders treat them as equals, whereas seventy-four percent *agreed* that it is important to them that Vietnamese church leaders treat them as equals. Two percent were *neutral*, no one selected *disagree*, and no one selected *strongly disagree* as their answer. The average score that Group B selected, based on SA=5, A=4, N=3, D=2, SD=1, is 4.22.

For Group C, Question 5A, the responses indicate that forty-six percent *strongly agreed* that it is important to them that Vietnamese church leaders treat them as equals, whereas fifty-two percent *agreed* that it is important to them that Vietnamese church leaders treat them as equals. Two percent were *neutral*, no one selected *disagree*, and no one selected *strongly disagree* as their answer. The average score that Group C selected, based on SA=5, A=4, N=3, D=2, SD=1, is 4.44.

The responses to Issue #5 (Q5 and Q5A): Treatment as Equals by Church Leaders are summarized in the following comparison chart.

Chart #5: The Younger Generation of Vietnamese are Treated as Equals by Church Leaders.

Question	Group A	Group B	Group C
5	4.64	1.16	1.26
5A	4.15	4.22	4.44

Issue #6 (Q6, Q6A): Ability to Relate to the Church's Vision of Reaching Vietnamese

On Question 6, for Group A, the responses indicate that thirty-two percent *strongly agreed* that during periods of regularly attending a Vietnamese church, they could relate to the church's vision, especially its vision for reaching Vietnamese unbelievers for Jesus Christ, whereas sixty-eight percent *agreed* that during periods of regularly attending a Vietnamese church, they could relate to the church's vision. No one selected *neutral*, no one selected *disagree*, and no one selected *strongly disagree* as their answer. The average score that Group A selected, based on SA=5, A=4, N=3, D=2, SD=1, is 4.32.

For Group B, Question 6, the responses indicate that ten percent *strongly disagreed* that during periods of regularly attending a Vietnamese church, they could relate to the church's vision, especially its vision for reaching Vietnamese unbelievers for Jesus Christ, whereas fifty percent *disagreed* that during periods of regularly attending a Vietnamese church, they could relate to the church's vision. Forty percent were *neutral*, no one selected *agree*, and no one selected *strongly agree* as their answer. The average score that Group B selected, based on SA=5, A=4, N=3, D=2, SD=1, is 2.3.

For Group C, Question 6, the responses indicate that fourteen percent *strongly disagreed* that during periods of regularly attending a Vietnamese church, they could relate to the church's vision, especially its vision for reaching Vietnamese unbelievers for Jesus Christ, whereas fifty-four percent *disagreed* that during periods of regularly attending a Vietnamese church, they could relate to the church's vision. Thirty-two percent were *neutral*, no one selected *agree*, and no one selected *strongly agree* as their answer. The average score that Group C selected, based on SA=5, A=4, N=3, D=2, SD=1, is 3.18.

On the additional Question 6A, for Group A, the responses indicate that sixty-eight percent *strongly agreed* that it is important to them that the church should reach out to Vietnamese unbelievers, whereas thirty-two percent *agreed* that it is important to them that the church should reach out to Vietnamese unbelievers. No one selected *neutral*, no one selected *disagree*, and no one selected *strongly disagree* as their answer. The average score that Group A selected, based on SA=5, A=4, N=3, D=2, SD=1, is 4.68.

For Group B, Question 6A, the responses indicate that thirty-two percent *strongly agreed* that it is important to them that the church should reach out to Vietnamese unbelievers, whereas sixty-six percent *agreed* that it is important to them that the church should reach out to Vietnamese unbelievers. Two percent were *neutral*, no one selected *disagree*, and no one selected *strongly disagree* as their answer. The average score that Group B selected, based on SA=5, A=4, N=3, D=2, SD=1, is 4.3.

For Group C, Question 6A, the responses indicate that seventy-two percent *strongly agreed* that it is important to them that the church should reach out to Vietnamese unbelievers, whereas twenty-eight percent *agreed* that it is important to them. No one selected *neutral*, no one selected *disagree*, and no one selected *strongly disagree* as their answer. The average score that Group C selected, based on SA=5, A=4, N=3, D=2, SD=1, is 4.72.

The findings for Issue #6 (Q6 and Q6A): Ability to Relate to the Vision of the Church is summarized in the following chart.

Chart #6: Ability to Relate to the Vision of the Church is summarized in the following chart, specifically its vision of reaching Vietnamese for Jesus Christ.

Question	Group A	Group B	Group C
6	4.32	2.3	3.18
6A	4.68	4.3	4.72

Issue #7 (Q7, Q7A): Importance of the Presence an English speaking Pastor

On Question 7, for Group A, the responses indicate that fifty-four percent *strongly agreed* that during periods of regularly attending a Vietnamese church, the presence of an English speaking pastor on staff would have enhanced their experience, whereas thirty-eight percent *agreed* that the presence of an English speaking pastor on staff would have enhanced their experience. Eight percent were *neutral*, no one selected *disagree*, and no one selected *strongly disagree* as their answer. The average score that Group A selected, based on SA=5, A=4, N=3, D=2, SD=1, is 4.46.

For Group B, Question 7, the responses indicate that only six percent *strongly agreed* that during periods of regularly attending a Vietnamese church, the presence of an English speaking pastor on staff would have enhanced their experience, whereas forty-eight percent *agreed* that the presence of an English speaking pastor on staff would have enhanced their experience. Forty-six percent were *neutral*, no one selected *disagreed*, and no one selected *strongly disagree* as their answer. The average score that Group B selected, based on SA=5, A=4, N=3, D=2, SD=1, is 3.6.

For Group C, Question 7, the responses indicate that twenty-six percent *strongly agreed* that during periods of regularly attending a Vietnamese church, the presence of an English speaking pastor on staff would have enhanced their experience, whereas sixty-eight percent *agreed* that the presence of an English speaking pastor on staff would have enhanced their experience. Six percent were *neutral*, no one selected *disagreed*, and no one selected *strongly disagree* as their answer. The average score that Group C selected, based on SA=5, A=4, N=3, D=2, SD=1, is 4.2.

On the additional Question 7A, for Group A, the responses indicate that seventy percent *strongly agreed* that it is important to them to have a pastor dedicated to the English-speaking ministry; an additional thirty percent *agreed* that it is important to them to have an English-speaking pastor. No other responses were selected for this question. The average score that Group A selected, based on SA=5, A=4, N=3, D=2, SD=1, is 4.7.

For Group B, Question 7A, the responses indicate that forty-two percent *strongly agreed* that it is important to them to have a pastor dedicated to an English-speaking ministry, whereas fifty-four percent *agreed* that it is important to them to have an English-speaking pastor. Four percent were *neutral*, no one selected *disagreed*, and no one selected *strongly disagree* as their answer. The average score that Group B selected, based on SA=5, A=4, N=3, D=2, SD=1, is 4.38.

For Group C, Question 7A, the responses indicate that twenty-four percent *strongly agreed* that it is important to them to have a pastor dedicated to an English-speaking ministry, whereas sixty percent *agreed* that it is important to them to have an English-speaking pastor. Sixteen percent were *neutral*, no one selected *disagreed*, and no one selected *strongly disagree* as their answer. The average score that Group C selected, based on SA=5, A=4, N=3, D=2, SD=1, is 4.08.

Comparison Chart #7 will summarize the findings regarding Issue #7 (Q7, Q7A): Importance of the Presence an English speaking Pastor.

Chart #7: Importance of the Presence an English speaking Pastor

Question	Group A	Group B	Group C
7	4.46	3.6	4.2
7A	4.7	4.38	4.08

CHAPTER 5

CONCLUSIONS

Issue #1: Performing tasks on a regular basis for the Sunday worship service

The results collected from the three participant groups in response to this question were surprisingly consistent: Group A had an average score of 4.42 (Q1)/4.06(Q1A), Group B had an average score of 4.42(Q1)/4.58(Q1A), and Group C had an average score of 4.56(Q1)/3.56(Q1A). These results demonstrate that all three groups were regularly involved in tasks for the Sunday worship service (4.42, 4.42, and 4.56). In addition, the first two groups agreed that this participation was important to them (4.06, 4.58); however, the third group average (3.56) suggests involvement in the Sunday worship service was somewhat less important to them. In summary, it does not appear that the responses to Issue #1 yield strong evidence that this is a factor in retention. The ones who left the church were as involved in the worship service as the ones who stayed; hence, the data is inconclusive.

Issue #2: Older Vietnamese valued my active involvement in church events

The responses to Issue #2 show much more variety. Group A had an average score of 4.58 (Q2)/4.64(Q2A), Group B had an average score of 1.3(Q2)/4.28(Q2A), and Group C had an average score of 1.38(Q2)/4.36(Q2A). The variation in these results opens the possibility that the participants in Group A (4.58) are retained because they believe the older Vietnamese valued their active involvement in the church events, whereas the other two groups (B, 1.3 and C, 1.38) strongly did not believe that the older Vietnamese valued their active involvement in the church events. Therefore, the data suggests that valuation of active involvement is an issue in retention since it was present in the retained group and not present in the non-retained groups. In other words, the data indicate that when the church leadership values the active involvement of the young people, this valuation may positively contribute to retention. In fact, all three groups (4.64, 4.28, 4.36) say that it is important to them that the older Vietnamese church leaders value their active involvement in church events.

Issue #3: My leadership abilities were valued by church leaders

The responses from Issue #3 showed similar variations as Issue #2, with Group A exhibiting an average score of 4.42 (Q3)/3.8(Q3A), Group B exhibiting an average score of 1.36(Q3)/4.34(Q3A), and Group C exhibiting an average score of 1.22(Q3)/4.34(Q3A). These results point to the likelihood that participants in Group A (4.42) are retained because during periods of regularly attending a Vietnamese church, they believed that their leadership abilities, whether they served in leadership or not, were valued by the church leaders, whereas the other two groups (B, 1.36, and C, 1.22) believed that during periods of regularly attending a Vietnamese church, their leadership abilities were not valued by church leaders. Given these results, Issue #3 also appears to contribute to the retention of young people in the church, especially since all three groups (3.8, 4.34, 4.34) indicated that it is important to them that Vietnamese church leaders value their leadership abilities.

Issue #4: Church leaders made it easy for me to talk about my spiritual needs

Responses to Issue #4 also show some differences between the three groups. Group A had an average score of 4.56 (Q4)/4.86(Q4A), Group B had an average score of 1.46(Q4)/4.64(Q4A), and Group C had an average score of 1.3(Q4)/1.38(Q4A). The results of Group A (4.56) suggest that these young people are retained because during periods of regularly attending a Vietnamese church, they believed that the church leaders made it easy for them to talk about their spiritual needs. Conversely, the other two groups (B, 1.46, and C, 1.3) believed that during periods of regularly attending a Vietnamese church, the church leaders did not made it easy for them to talk about their spiritual needs. In addition, only two groups (A, 4.86 and B, 4.64) say that it is important to them that they can talk to church leaders about their spiritual needs. However, Group C (1.38), those participants who no longer attend church, indicated that it was not important to them to talk to church leaders about their spiritual needs. The data suggests that the ability to talk to church leaders about their spiritual needs is an important concern for those who continue to attend church, but not for those who have dropped out of church. In other words, for those who remained committed to God and church, it is an important issue, and for those who are not committed to God and church, it does not appear to be significant.

Issue #5: Vietnamese church leaders treated me as their equals

Responses to Issue #5 also revealed variation across the groups. Group A averaged 4.64 (Q5)/4.5(Q5A), Group B averaged 1.16(Q5)/4.22(Q5A), and Group C averaged 1.26(Q5)/4.44(Q5A). Group A (4.64), the participants who remained in the Vietnamese church, indicated that during periods of regularly attending a Vietnamese church, they believed that they were treated by church leaders as their equals, whereas the other groups (B, 1.16 and C, 1.26) felt that during periods of regularly attending a Vietnamese church, they did not believe that they were treated as equals by church leaders. As the matter of fact, all three groups (4.15, 4.22, 4.44) say that it is important to them that Vietnamese church leaders treat them as equals. In other words, the data responses to this issue suggest a strong relationship between retention and the perception of being treated as an equal.

Issue #6: Could relate to the church's vision, especially its vision of reaching Vietnamese for Jesus Christ

The responses to Issue #6 also offered interesting insights. Group A had an average score of 4.32 (Q6)/4.68(Q6A), Group B had an average score of 2.3(Q6)/4.3(Q6A), and Group C had an average score of 3.18(Q6)/4.72(Q6A). These results indicate that perhaps part of the reason that participants in Group A (4.32) are retained is that during periods of regularly attending a Vietnamese church, they could relate to the church's vision, especially its vision of reaching Vietnamese for Jesus Christ, whereas the unretained groups (B, 2.3 and C, 3.18) say that during periods of regularly attending a Vietnamese church, they could not relate to the church's vision, especially its vision of reaching Vietnamese for Jesus Christ. Indeed, all three groups (4.68, 4.3, 4.72) seemed to indicate that being able to relate to the vision of the church and reaching Vietnamese for Jesus Christ is important to them. In other words, the data suggests being able to relate to the church's vision of reaching Vietnamese is an issue in retention.

Issue #7: Importance of having an English-speaking pastor on staff

Lastly, Issue #7 had the following results: Group A averaged 4.46(Q7)/4.7(Q7A), Group B averaged 3.6(Q7)/4.38(Q7A), and Group C averaged 4.2(Q7)/4.08(Q7A). Groups A and C (4.46, 4.2) indicated that during periods of regularly attending a Vietnamese church, they believed that having an English-speaking pastor dedicated to English-speaking ministries on staff enhanced their experience, whereas the score for Group B (3.6) was somewhat lower. Even though the scores for all three groups (A, 4.7, 4.38, 4.08) show that having a pastor dedicated to English speaking ministries is important to them, the data reveals no significant differences between those who were retained and those who were not retained. Thus, having a pastor dedicated to English-speaking ministries did not appear to have a significant effect on retention. The responses to Issue 7 were inconclusive regarding retention.

A concise summary of the results of the survey:

Issue	Conclusion
Issue #1: Performing tasks on a regular basis for the Sunday worship service	Data is inconclusive regarding the impact on retention
Issue #2: Valuation of older Vietnamese valued my active involvement in church events	Data is conclusive regarding the impact on retention.
Issue #3: Members of the younger generation believed that their leadership abilities were valued by church leaders	Data is conclusive regarding the impact on retention.
Issue #4: Church leaders made it easy for members of the younger generation to talk about their spiritual needs	Data indicates that this is a significant factor for those who remain church attenders, but not for those who stopped attending church.
Issue #5: Vietnamese Church Leaders treated members of the younger generation as their equals	Data is conclusive regarding the impact on retention.
Issue #6: Ability to relate to the church's vision, especially its vision of reaching Vietnamese for Jesus Christ	Data is suggestive, but not conclusive, for an impact on retention.

Issue #7: Presence of an English-speaking pastor dedicated to English-Speaking ministries	Data is inconclusive regarding the impact on retention

Ultimately, the purpose of this research is to analyze the relationship between feelings of valuation from church leadership and the rate of retention of the younger generation in Vietnamese immigrant churches. The results of the SGVFG Scale Survey reveal that Issues #2, #3, and #5 show a strong relationship with retention. In other words, an attitude of valuing younger potential leaders by acknowledging their active involvement in church and receiving them as equals could be an opportunity to yield a high rate of the retention of the second generation in Vietnamese churches.

REFLECTIONS ON THE IMPLICATIONS OF THE SURVEY DATA

Since Vietnamese church leaders and pastors are heavily influenced by a high power distance culture, which they have imported and implemented in the church setting for over one hundred years, the children's ministry is frequently considered less significant and less important. As a result, the children's ministry is separated from the church's regular worship service every Sunday. According to Ivy Beckwith in *Postmodern Children's Ministry*, this creates a situation in which the children are not able to experience what it means to be in the presence of God and what it means to praise God alongside others at church during the main service.[121] Likewise, the second generation young people seem to feel that their participation in the services and ministry of the church are often unacknowledged and unappreciated by their church leaders and pastors. In other words, the second generation of Vietnamese who come to church on Sunday with their parents are not considered by the church leadership to be significant part of the faith community.

The responses to questions 2 and 2A, especially from those who are attending non-Vietnamese churches or not attending church at all, reflect that the first generation of Vietnamese have failed to adequately communicate that they value the efforts and contributions of the second generation to their church services. In other words, the first generation of Vietnamese in a congregation have continued to practice their culturally-ingrained high power distance relationships persistently for more than forty years in the United States, causing conflict and misunderstanding from the younger generation's perspective and building a major gap between the first and the second generations. In *Change it Up*, Dale Edwardson properly discerns that many churches today are trying to create programs and systems instead of making disciples,

---

[121] Ivy Beckwith, *Postmodern Children's Ministry: Ministry to Children in the 21ˢᵗ Century* (Grand Rapids, Michigan: Zondervan, 2004), 79-80.

The Relationship Between Second Generation Leaders' Sense of Valuation

which allows them to remain comfortable and satisfied as closed communities, protected from the cruel world outside the church.[122]

According to Edwardson's citation of Dr. Ron Walborn, the Dean of Alliance Theological Seminary at Nyack College, American churches today are actively seeking a way to break free from the "consumer culture" that has been created over the past thirty years. If this is the case, then it will likely take tremendous efforts for second-generation Vietnamese leaders to break free from the "consumer culture" that Vietnamese churches worldwide have been perpetuating for over one hundred years. In addition, Paul Rutledge, the author of *The Role of Religion in Ethnic Self-Identity*, states that Vietnamese tradition and culture, based on the worldview of Confucianism, have molded Vietnamese society for more than two thousand years (since Vietnam was established) and have also impacted religious practices in Vietnam.[123] This tradition and culture have misled many Vietnamese Christians to come to church simply because they are going to a nice place to enjoy a performance. Dr. Walborn expresses his concern that the American "consumer culture" has created a generation of passive disciples who are no longer impacting their neighborhood, their culture,

---

[122] Dale H. Edwardson, *Change it up: Transforming Ordinary Churches into Passionate Disciplemaking Comminities* (Maitland, Florida: Xulonpress, 2013), 73.

[123] Paul Rutledge, *The Role of Religion in Ethnic Self-Identity: A Vietnamese Community* (Lanham, MD; University Press of America, 19850, 24-26.

and their world surrounding them.[124] The same process is likely taking place in the Vietnamese churches in America due to the American "consumer culture" combined with the remnants of the influence of Confucianism.

The responses to questions 3 and 3A, especially from those who are attending non-Vietnamese churches or not attending church at all, reflect the younger generation's belief that the Vietnamese church leaders and pastors seem to devalue the contributions of the potential leaders from among the second-generation Vietnamese. Ironically, despite feeling devalued, the younger generation remains very willing to serve, creating a situation in which there is ample opportunity for the first generation of Vietnamese leaders and pastors to train and to equip the second-generation Vietnamese who have been raised in the United States.

In fact, Edwardson believes that many churches today fail to experience healthy growth because they tend to attract nominal believers who are bored with church programs. This traditional church environment is likely to appeal to more believers just like the ones who already attend and is unlikely to attract unbelievers. Church leaders and pastors today often overlook the important aspects of what the kingdom of God

---

[124] Dale H. Edwardson, *Change it up: Transforming Ordinary Churches into Passionate Disciplemaking Comminities* (Maitland, Florida: Xulonpress, 2013), vii.

should look like, perhaps because they may be either uninformed or indifferent toward God's purposes for the church.[125]

The responses to questions 4 and 4A, especially from those who are attending non-Vietnamese churches or not attending church at all, reflect that the younger generation did not believe that it was easy for them to talk about their spiritual needs to their Vietnamese church leaders. It seems that the Vietnamese church leaders and pastors have failed to develop the communication skills necessary to facilitate relationships with second generation members in order to discern and meet their spiritual needs. The problems facing the youth have not been addressed, and their participation at church has been overlooked simply because church leaders and pastors from the first generation have not developed and maintained their lines of communication with the younger ones who have different ideals and different perspectives.

Unfortunately, many first generation leaders and pastors in the Vietnamese immigrant churches may have lost their opportunity to develop a meaningful relationship between the second generation potential leaders and themselves. Martin Sanders, the author of *The Power of Mentoring*, believes that church leaders should develop a spiritual relationship with the younger leaders by asking questions and listening to them, thereby creating a healthy friendship which will

---

[125] Dale H. Edwardson, *Change It Up: Transforming Ordinary Churches into Passionate Disciplemaking Comminities* (Maitland, Florida: Xulon Press, 2013), 76.

nurture the development of godly character.[126] Yet today, cultural setting and tradition remain stumbling blocks that make the second generation of Vietnamese Christians feel that talking and sharing their spiritual needs with their church leaders is like talking to their boss instead of a friend and partner in ministry.

The responses to questions 5 and 5A, especially from those who are attending non-Vietnamese churches or not attending church at all, demonstrate that it is important to these young people that the Vietnamese church leaders treat them as equals. Unfortunately, church administration and staff positions are rarely offered to the younger Vietnamese potential leaders; however, these positions would provide opportunities to engage them in a leadership environment as well as to prepare them for future Christian vocations. As previously mentioned, Vietnamese culture and its traditions fall into a high power index category, and many of the first-generation Vietnamese leaders and pastors have propagated this influence in the church setting for their own benefit.[127]

The responses to Questions 6 and 6A, especially from those who are attending non-Vietnamese churches or not attending church at all,

---

[126] Martin Sanders, *The Power of Mentoring: Shaping People Who Will Shape the World* (Camp Hill, Pennsylvania: Christian Publications, Inc. 2004), 26-27.

[127] Geert Hofstede, Gert Jan Hofstede and Michael Minkov, *Cultures and Organizations: Software of the Mind-Intercultural Cooperation and Its Importance for Survival* (New York: McGraw Hill, 2010), 20.

reflect an unfortunate situation in which the first-generation church leaders, pastors, and parents have neglected to transmit a meaningful vision for ministry. Instead, they have been using the church facility as a meeting place for social gatherings and using the church service as a platform for displaying power over one another. In addition, many first-generation Vietnamese church leaders and members have been using the church platform to promote traditional events in which the performer's outfit may be the most important feature on the day of the church event. Children are also encouraged to dress in very nice outfits for their performances; thus, the true vision and purpose for the church is often vague to the children. Ashish Raichur, the founder and director of Frontier Missions, has published an article sharing his burden that many churches have failed to see the dangers in the lives of their younger generations who face tremendous tensions outside the church, and thus, churches today have become powerless since they have become primarily places for social gatherings and forums for cultural expression with only a tinge of spirituality.[128]

In other words, many church programs do not reflect God's priority to reach unreached people, and the younger Vietnamese generations do not really see a reason to come to church with their parents every

---

[128] Ashish Raichur, "The Second Generation: Spiritual and Cultural Conflicts," n.p. (01/07/2009) *Agape Partners International*. Cited 2 February 2015. Online: http://agapepartners.org/articles/34/1/The-Second-GenerationSpiritual-and-Cultural-Conflicts/Page1.html.

Sunday, where their ideas and their needs are seldom heard by their parents or their church leaders. Ironically, the language barrier does not appear to be the main factor in declining youth retention; rather, a poor and vague promotion of the church's vision for outreach program may be the responsible factor.

Channing Johnson is absolutely right as he provides the critique that first-generation churchgoers today have a bad reputation among the young because they are unaware of the characteristics and concerns of the younger post-modern generations. Instead, first-generation churchgoers seem to want to take credit for getting their children to church to convert them, but they rarely have an interest in dialog, listening, or sharing with their younger ones.[129]

The responses to Questions 7 and 7A, especially from those who are attending non-Vietnamese churches or not attending church at all, reflect that the hiring of an English speaking pastor is itself an act of valuation of the second generation. However, they are not so concerned with whether their church leaders or pastors speak Vietnamese or English. More importantly, they would like to see a cohesive vision from their leaders or pastors that they could embrace and that would enable them to become a partner in the mission of their church. In other words, communication between the first and the second generation is

---

[129] R. Channing Johnson, *Where Have All the Young People Gone: Exploring Generational Change and How Young People Can be Reached* (Glendale, Arizona: 2012), 105-107.

one of the crucial elements for closing the gap of misunderstanding between the two parties. Tod Bolsinger, in *It Takes a Church to Raise a Christian*, has shared some important issues that could positively impact the rate of the younger generation's retention. He maintains that a church has to accept their younger ones just as they are and to welcome them as part of the community. He further suggests that when a church congregation begins to treat others, including those in the younger generations, as their equals, it will help to heal painful brokenness and will transform the community into more than the church today could ever imagine.[130]

On the positive side, the results of the SGVFG Scale Survey from those who are still attending the Vietnamese church and Montagnard churches show that engaging the younger generations in leadership promises a high retention rate of the younger generation within the Vietnamese immigrant churches in the United States. This paper's author, a researcher himself and a senior pastor at a Vietnamese church in Raleigh, North Carolina, has regularly interacted with the church youth and invited them into staff discussions, highlighting one way to enhance their church involvement in the Sunday service. The outcome of engaging younger potential leaders has transformed the entire

---

[130] Tod E. Bolsinger, *It Takes a Church to Raise a Christian: How Community of God Transforms Lives* (Grand Rapids, Michigan: Brazos Press, 2004), 22.

congregation, especially when one particular younger leader began to lead others within his own group.

Even though this one particular leader has been recognized by his pastor and church staff, this pastor has maintained regular discussions with his other young potential staff through Bible studies and sharing the church's vision before praying together during the week. In fact, during discussion time with the youth, this pastor often listens to the youth's needs and discusses their methodologies for reaching other young people through the church. In addition, during the church staff meetings, potential leaders from the second generation are invited to observe and to share what they believe their church can do in order to attract the younger generations within the church to be involved in the church's overall ministry.

In return, the pastor urges all parents in the church to support their children when they are invited to participate in youth outreach events that have been established by the church staff in cooperation with the youth. In supporting the children, parents must commit to bringing their children to church on designated days to prepare for youth events. This pastor further advocates that at times the youth event should be allowed to happen during the Sunday service as a main event instead of as a supplement.

From his own experience, his thorough literature review, and from the conclusions provided by the survey, the researcher identifies four primary characteristics that are present in many Vietnamese churches and which seem to be responsible for the failure of many churches to retain their younger congregants. The first factor is the autocratic manner in which many Vietnamese pastors oversee their churches. This characteristic is likely a carryover within their generation from their days under Communism and from their high power distance culture. The second factor is closely related to the first: cronyism among the pastors. In other words, they tend to prefer and promote leaders from within their generation. This results in limited opportunities for young leaders to serve. The third factor is the apparent lack vision for nurturing the youth in order to preserve the church for future generations. Fourthly, significant barriers seem to exist between many first-generation pastors and the young people in their churches.

CHURCH RECOMMENDATIONS

Cultural differences and conflicts between the first and the second generation of Vietnamese within the church cannot be ignored if the first generation of Vietnamese is committed to seeing the younger generation continue to grow spiritually and become actively involved in church discipleship. It is necessary for the first generation of Vietnamese pastors to consider every Sunday service as a missional opportunity to intentionally and meaningfully engage the younger generations in the church activities in order for them to be trained as effective servant leaders within the church.

Within the current Vietnamese church setting, cultural activities which appeal primarily to the first generation of Vietnamese should be transformed into a training school model where potential younger leaders can be integrated into church leadership. This change would provide more opportunity for the younger generation to learn and share their perspectives in regard to their spiritual needs and would create an environment which may yield a greater retention of the second generation within the church.

Since the second generation of Vietnamese is largely bilingual, they have the language ability to gather in mentoring relationships with their first generation leaders, so they can learn God's word under the rule of Christ. This, in turn, allows them to serve and to teach others within their groups at church.[131] In addition, the second generation of Vietnamese typically will build more friendships outside of the church after they are trained as disciple-makers for Christ. Their likelihood of developing more relationships outside the church than the older

---

[131] London Confession (1644), Baptist Confession of Faith, 2nd, rev. ed., ed. William L. Lumpkin, rev. Bill J. Leonard (Valley Forge, Pa.: Judson Press, 2011), 143.

generation has the potential to widen the influence of the church in the community.

Furthermore, in many immigrant churches today, the first generation leaders often encourage the younger generation to focus on school and their careers rather than on becoming disciples within the church. This situation can become a barrier between the two generations and can result in a misunderstanding of each other's spiritual needs. Instead, first generation church leaders should see the value of church activities and church community so that the church creates a unique environment which church members view as a second family. Church can be a place to produce many godly men and women for the world when church leaders utilize such opportunities to proclaim biblical preaching and teaching instead of lecturing on their own precepts; otherwise, church leaders will turn the whole church into a secular entertainment agency which will corrupt religion.

Another factor that can help the immigrant church today to stay focused on developing Christ-like disciples is to train the younger generation of Vietnamese Americans and merge them into church leadership. In order to do this, the young people must begin to learn the Bible and to think biblically from an early age, both at church and at home. Frank outlaw quotes:

"Watch your thoughts; they become words. Watch your words; they become actions. Watch your actions; they become habits. Watch your habits; they become character. Watch your character; it becomes your destiny."[132]

Developing the younger generation of Vietnamese into biblically healthy and godly Christians requires lot of time and energy from church leaders as well as from church parents. The church must provide a productive environment to teach and to support the second generation of Vietnamese as they develop their leadership abilities within the church. However, the responsibility for developing church leaders does not lie completely within the church. Christian parents must also support the young developing leaders.

Another opportunity for the younger generation of Vietnamese to develop their potential leadership while they are still under their parents' supervision and the church's leadership is to allow them to participate in church programs that fit their capabilities and talents since the majority of Vietnamese Americans are well trained through their middle and high schools in the American school system. For example, many Vietnamese Americans today are gifted in playing musical instruments as well as playing characters in theater; thus, they can be encouraged to use these gifts to perform at church where they are often excited

---

[132] Frank Outlaw, "Goodreads," Cited 14 August 2015. Online: http://www.goodreads.com/author/quotes/13466663.Frank_Outlaw.

The Relationship Between Second Generation Leaders' Sense of Valuation

to serve when their abilities have been acknowledged and they have been received and treated as equal partners in ministry by their parents and church leaders.

The first generation leaders must make every effort to listen to and meet the needs of the younger generations who remain committed to the Vietnamese church, or they run the risk of losing them. The young people who are involved in church leadership should be invited to sit with the church staff and elders and should be encouraged to voice their spiritual and personal needs so that the first generation can discern where to focus their efforts in meeting the needs of the younger generation. Since most of young people in the Vietnamese second generation are either born or raised in America, they see the world from a different perspective than their parents do; thus, it is necessary for their concerns to be heard so that the older leaders can understand the challenges they face outside of their homes and can seek to provide what the young people need to support their spiritual formation. These types of open discussions across generations have the potential to reap a lasting benefit within the immigrant churches across the U.S. In order words, humble, genuine, and conciliatory conversations will signify to the younger Vietnamese that the older generation is ready to welcome them as full partners in the church and is committed to training them as God's servant leaders, which is in according with the will of God.

Immigrant pastors and church leaders, including parents who are part of the first generation in America, should initiate an evaluation of their church situation by asking themselves difficult questions about why their second generation children often decide not to return to their parents' churches after college. They need to realistically and unselfishly consider the steps that are necessary to make room for the active participation of the next generation in church leadership. The time is now for the first generation of church leaders and pastors to soften their commanding voices and listen to the vision and ambitions of the younger generation for the church.

The nature of these supplemental church activities may depend on the church geography; church leaders and parents will be able to identify the activities that will be most effective in engaging their younger generation in the church setting. For example, some churches do not have younger people who are skillful in theater or music performance, but they might have many youth who are good at outdoor spots. In this case, church leaders can provide an opportunity for their youth to participate in a sports ministry to which they can invite their friends from their schools or neighborhoods to participate.

In parts of America where church leaders might not have enough skilled members to create theater productions or develop sports ministries, church leaders should start from what they have by focusing on teaching and training the youngest members within their capabilities and talents; even a small group of young people is able to grow into healthy Christians who are living according to biblical principles. Church leaders in smaller churches should not feel that there is nothing they can do to appeal to the younger generation. In fact, it takes very little resources to incorporate high-tech communication into church programs; church programs can be posted through Instagram, Twister, Facebook, Snapchat, and Tango in order to make connections with people outside the church. The younger generation of Vietnamese youth today is very skilled with these modern technologies and can help their church leaders to promote church programs to outsiders.

Another example of a way that the church can incorporate younger people into ministry is by organizing a short-term mission trip for dental students and dentists, medical students, or nurses to participate on behalf of the church to provide medical assistance once a year to the neighborhood in which the church is located, where such a ministry will bring a meaningful message both to the community and to the younger generation of Vietnamese. In other words, the first generation of Vietnamese leaders can effectively bridge the gap between the first and the second generation by endorsing their abilities and careers as valuable and beneficial ways to serve within a healthy church family.

As the matter of fact, the researcher himself has carefully adapted one of his suggestions above into reality where he lives and works and has successfully applied this strategy into his church setting and community after many years of serving at his church. Such an endeavor requires a lot of energy and many hours in prayer, as well as spending time with church staff and church members to ensure a plan that is according to God's will.

CONCLUDING REFLECTIONS

After more than three years of serving within the Vietnamese congregation and the Montagnard community in Raleigh, North Carolina, from 2013 and 2015, the researcher has had the opportunity to successfully implement his seminary studies into his church's daily practice. He has been able to develop an environment where potential leaders among the younger generation are highly recognized and engaged in church leadership. One of the most engaging elements, which has led to successful youth participation and has promise for a high retention rate of the younger generation, has involved transferring the church's gospel outreach responsibility to the younger generation.

As a result of valuing and treating the younger generation as equal participants in the church leadership, many of the young people from the Vietnamese church in Raleigh, including the Montagnard church, have successfully established a musical drama program in which the younger generation is using their talents to reflect the message of Christ through their musical programs. Through this emerging ministry, a young leader and his team have been recognized by the church leaders and staff, have grown spiritually, and have become a crucial connection in closing the cultural gap between the first and the second generations.

Effective communication has been the primary instrument in this journey. The opportunity for church leaders and younger potential leaders to share ideas and pray together has helped to eliminate cultural barriers and misunderstandings. In other words, when a spiritual leader builds opportunities to share his daily spiritual walk with Christ through reading God's word and praying with a younger leader, he empowers the younger leader to be raised up biblically, and he will be able to turn around and train many others by challenging them to live for Christ and to witness for Christ among unbelievers. The whole congregation is inspired seeing that their children and young adults have begun to live biblically both at home and at school. Furthermore, parents have begun to see that a faithful commitment to their children's regular involvement at church-planned outreach programs has transformed their own perceptions of church involvement, resulting in a trust that the church can produce spiritually healthy individuals.

The ultimate purpose of the SGVFG Scale Survey that the researcher designed for this research study was to identify the possible factors which might contribute favorably to a higher retention rate of the younger generation in the Vietnamese church. However, in the course of implementing what he was learning in his studies, this pastor discovered that when a pastor starts to focus on God's people and purposefully engages people of all ages in the church's ministry at their own levels, both generations are able to resolve misconceptions between the two cultures and become godly partners, helping each other to grow spiritually. Carey Nieuwhof, in *Nine Surefire Ways to Make Your Church Completely Ineffective*, perceptively identifies a danger wherein church leaders become self-focused, which has the potential to destroy the very nature of the mission of God's church. In other words, when leaders and pastors focus on themselves instead of others, they become self-absorbed, and nobody enjoys spending time with them. If people do not enjoy spending time with the church leaders, they will view spending time at church in the same way.[133]

The researcher also identified another factor which he has unintentionally implemented in his own church and promises the possibility of increasing the retention of the younger generation. That factor is trust.

---

[133] Carey Nieuwhof, "Nine Surefire Ways to Make Your Church Completely Ineffective," n.p. Cited 9 February 2015. Online: http://www.churchleaders.com/pastors/pastor-articles/246803-9-surefire-ways-make-church-completely-ineffective.html.

When younger potential leaders are trusted and when they are invited to share in the authority of the church, they will take their responsibility seriously before God, which will cultivate their desire to move closer to God through their daily spiritual walk, along with their church leaders. The researcher also has seen that when he faithfully gives himself up before the Lord and asks Christ to lead him as he is called to lead Christ's church, God will use him to bring more godly people into the church's vocational ministry. As a result, after three years of integrating the younger leaders from the congregation into the service of the church, four younger leaders out of fifty young people have already decided to enter seminary for further training because God has transformed them to be able to see the needs within their generation, and they want to be his servants in the near future.

Ultimately, the church is not a place for maintaining a particular culture, nor is it a place for upholding the glory of individuals and preserving memories of the past. The church is the body of Christ where each individual, in both the first and the second generations of Vietnamese, should be trained to become Christ's disciples. Furthermore, church is not a place for church leaders and pastors to exercise their individual power over their congregations; rather, church is meant to be a second family of God's people who were once lost but are now found in the blood of Jesus Christ. Furthermore, church is a place where Christians are trained before sending them out to witness for Christ among their relatives, their neighbors, their co-workers, their schoolmates, and the world.

For further research, if it is true that the church is a second family of believers whom Christ has selected and called to become his disciples, then every member of a congregation should to start with his or her own family and institute "family worship," to help prepare each member to be sent out to fulfill Christ's Great Commission. Strategy and methodology should be studied by church leaders and pastors in order to turn their churches into training centers to produce spiritual politicians, spiritual medical doctors, spiritual engineers, spiritual laborers, and so on. Church leaders and pastors should be the primary examples in this spiritual household to lead their congregations so that the entire church can become a spiritual people to witness to their neighborhoods and to the world.

In fact, in order for a church to produce spiritual believers of Christ, church leaders and pastors, including their entire households, should provide a spiritual model of family worship prior to leading the rest of their congregation. Therefore, vocational ministry within the church should be distinguished as God's sacred task, which differs from a secular career. In order to determine if a person should engage in vocational ministry for God's kingdom, it is necessary that a person's entire household should also be called.

In Smith's hypothesis, he believes that programs that prepare every church member for service are crucially important because, according to Schaller's observation, both heritage ties and current ministries and missions of a particular congregation have the potential to generate high levels of member satisfaction.[134] In other words, there will be a higher rate of younger generation retention within the Vietnamese churches nationwide when the whole church becomes a missional family, where every single member, both old and new, is encouraged to be involved in the church's activities. There should be many roles within a church that pastors and leaders can share with other members in their congregations, according to Smith's observation. A job assignment or any program that involves families with young children is likely to be important because church members tend to participate with family responsibility as part of their call to serve.[135]

Further research into the retention of young people in the church is necessary because it is important to God for everybody, including young people, to meditate on God's word day and night, since God's

---

[134] Donald P. Smith, *The Mainstream Protestant* "Decline": *The Presbyterian Pattern.* eds. Milton J. Coalter, John M. Mulder, and Louis B. Weeks, (Louisville, Kentucky: Westminster/John Knox Press, 1990), 92

[135] Ibid., 93.

believers are his chosen people. God has consistently demonstrated his care for the younger generations, as far back as when the Israelites were called out of Egypt under Moses' guidance and God had commanded every adult, according to Deuteronomy 6:7-9, saying, "Impress [these words] on your children. Talk about them when you sit at home and when you walk along the road, when you lie down and when you get up. Tie them as symbols on your hands and bind them on your foreheads. Write them on the doorframes of your houses and on your gates."

Jesus also demonstrated how he cared for little children, when he said that heaven belongs to them (Mk. 10:13-16). In following Jesus' example, the church today should take seriously each individual's walk with Christ, such that each family member, including children, should reflect Christ-likeness and have the potential to be a spiritual leader, starting from the church leaders' and pastors' families and reaching to every church member's family, as every believer is called to be the light of the world.

Finally, attaining a higher retention rate of the younger generation within the Vietnamese church nationwide will require pastors to be humble servants of God and include others in their daily spiritual journeys with God. Having a vision and passion for the Great Commission are further requirements for church leaders and pastors in order for the work of the Holy Spirit to transform their lives and the lives of others.

Communicating effectively and engaging others in church leadership will also help to nurture many younger potential leaders to continue to follow in their leaders' and pastors' steps. In other words, the commitment and dedication of leaders and pastors to their sacred task, the church vocational ministry that has been entrusted to them by God, will enable the first generation and the second generation to stand together for Christ.

APPENDIX A

SGVFG SCALE

<u>Details</u>

SA = (5) Strongly Agree

A = (4) Agree

N = (3) Neutral

D = (2) Disagree

SD = (1) Strongly Disagree

1. During periods of regularly attending a Vietnamese church, I was actively performing tasks on a regular basis for the Sunday worship service.

SA   A   N   D   SD

1A: It is important to me that I am actively performing tasks on a regular basis for the Sunday worship service.

SA   A   N   D   SD

2. During periods of regularly attending a Vietnamese church, I believe(d) older Vietnamese valued my active involvement in church events

SA   A   N   D   SD

2A: It is important to me that the older Vietnamese valued my active involvement in church events.

SA   A   N   D   SD

3. During periods of regularly attending a Vietnamese church, I believe(d) my leadership abilities, whether I served in leadership or not, were valued by church leaders.

SA   A   N   D   SD

3A: It is important to me that Vietnamese church leaders value my leadership abilities.

SA   A   N   D   SD

4. During periods of regularly attending a Vietnamese church, I believe(d) the church leaders made it easy for me to talk to them about my spiritual needs.

SA   A   N   D   SD

4A: It is important to me that I can talk to church leaders freely about my spiritual needs.

SA   A   N   D   SD

5. During periods of regularly attending a Vietnamese church, I believe(d) I was treated by church leaders as their equals.

SA   A   N   D   SD

5A: It is important to me that Vietnamese church leaders treat me as their equals.

SA   A   N   D   SD

6. During periods of regularly attending a Vietnamese church, I can (could) relate to the church's vision, especially its vision of reaching Vietnamese for Jesus Christ.

SA   A   N   D   SD

6A: It is important to me that reaching Vietnamese for Jesus Christ is priority.

SA   A   N   D   SD

7. During periods of regularly attending a Vietnamese church, I believe(d) having an English pastor dedicated to English-speaking ministries on staff enhanced (would have enhanced) my experience.

SA   A   N   D   SD

7A: Having a speaking pastor dedicated to English-speaking ministries is important to me.

SA   A   N   D   SD

APPENDIX B

Vietnamese Evangelical Church (C&MA)
6501 Fox Rd.
Raleigh, NC 27616
Tel: (919) 649-4175

Pastor Nhiem Thai Tran

August 20th 2014

Dear Mr(s). _____,

I am a doctoral student at Alliance Theological Seminary, New York, and I am conducting a research project for my doctoral dissertation this year for a Doctoral program.

The purpose of this study is to analyze the impact of effectively merging potential leaders from the younger Vietnamese generation into church leadership, and the effect of this practice on the church's retention of the younger generation. The results of the study will show that engaging the younger Vietnamese generations in leadership is a necessary approach for making disciples within the immigrant Vietnamese community. The reason for this study arose out of an intergenerational conflict which has existed for some years between the first and second generations of Vietnamese church leaders and members. Thus, the researcher proposes that merging potential leaders of the younger Vietnamese generation into church leadership will increase retention of the younger generation in the Vietnamese churches.

Therefore, I would like to have you return my survey through e-mail and I will keep your responses in my church office as confidential. It would be great if you can submit your responses before October 30th, 2014 so that I could have all data analysis ready for my dissertation.

Please feel free to email me of call me if you have any questions.

Sincerely,

Rev.Trần Thái Nhiệm

Senior Pastor

APPENDIX C

Survey Participants in Group A – Vietnamese Alliance Church and Montagnard
Alliance church members under the South Atlantic District of the C&MA

Number of Participants	Age of Participants	Years in Church	Denomination C&MA
1	16	10	Vietnamese Church
2	18	10	Vietnamese Church
3	17	05	Vietnamese Church
4	18	05	Vietnamese Church
5	18	06	Vietnamese Church
6	19	07	Vietnamese Church
7	20	07	Vietnamese Church
8	20	08	Vietnamese Church
9	20	15	Vietnamese Church
10	21	12	Vietnamese Church
11	24	12	Vietnamese Church
12	25	07	Vietnamese Church
13	26	08	Vietnamese Church
14	26	08	Vietnamese Church
15	26	10	Vietnamese Church
16	25	09	Vietnamese Church
17	24	13	Vietnamese Church
18	22	17	Vietnamese Church
19	22	05	Vietnamese Church
20	23	05	Montagnard Church
21	25	05	Montagnard Church
22	23	06	Montagnard Church

23	17	10	Montagnard Church
24	18	10	Montagnard Church
25	19	17	Montagnard Church
26	19	16	Montagnard Church
27	19	10	Montagnard Church
28	20	11	Montagnard Church
29	20	12	Montagnard Church
30	21	13	Montagnard Church
31	22	10	Montagnard Church
32	22	06	Montagnard Church
33	23	08	Montagnard Church
34	24	09	Montagnard Church
35	24	11	Montagnard Church
36	21	10	Montagnard Church
37	22	10	Montagnard Church
38	21	15	Montagnard Church
39	18	10	Montagnard Church
40	19	15	Montagnard Church
41	23	12	Vietnamese Church
42	24	10	Vietnamese Church
43	25	19	Vietnamese Church
44	25	18	Vietnamese Church
45	22	15	Vietnamese Church
46	21	16	Vietnamese Church
47	21	18	Vietnamese Church
48	20	10	Vietnamese Church
49	20	10	Vietnamese Church
50	22	10	Vietnamese Church
Total Participants	Average Age	Average Years	
	21.4	10.62	

APPENDIX D

Survey Participants in Group B – Those who once attended a Vietnamese Church but are now attending non-Vietnamese Churches

Number of Participants	Age of Participants	Years in Vietnamese Church	Denomination
1	22	5	Southern Baptist Church
2	22	6	Southern Baptist Church
3	23	5	Southern Baptist Church
4	25	6	Southern Baptist Church
5	26	5	Southern Baptist Church
6	26	6	Southern Baptist Church
7	22	9	Southern Baptist Church
8	21	5	Southern Baptist Convention
9	21	8	Southern Baptist Convention
10	20	5	Southern Baptist Convention
11	25	8	Southern Baptist Convention
12	26	5	Evangelical Lutheran Church
13	26	4	Evangelical Lutheran Church
14	27	7	Evangelical Lutheran Church
15	29	8	Evangelical Lutheran Church
16	23	5	Calvary Chapel
17	25	5	Calvary Chapel
18	25	2	Methodist Church
19	25	5	Methodist Church
20	25	2	Methodist Church
21	25	4	Calvary Chapel
22	26	6	Calvary Chapel

23	26	4	Methodist Church
24	25	5	Methodist Church
25	24	9	Assemblies of God
26	24	6	Assemblies of God
27	20	8	Assemblies of God
28	20	9	Assemblies of God
29	19	8	Assemblies of God
30	19	6	Assemblies of God
31	20	4	Assemblies of God
32	20	5	Assemblies of God
33	21	4	Assemblies of God
34	21	6	Assemblies of God
35	21	7	Assemblies of God
36	25	6	Methodist Church
37	25	4	Methodist Church
38	24	6	Methodist Church
39	26	3	Methodist Church
40	24	4	Methodist Church
41	23	8	Methodist Church
42	21	9	Presbyterian Church
43	20	5	Presbyterian Church
44	21	5	Evangelical Lutheran Church
45	22	9	Evangelical Lutheran Church
46	20	6	Evangelical Lutheran Church
47	23	4	The Episcopal Church
48	20	3	Churches of Christ
49	22	7	Pentecostal Assemblies of the World
50	26	5	Evangelical Lutheran Church
Total Participants	Average Age	Average Years	
	23.14	5.72	

APPENDIX E

Survey Participants in Group C – Those who have not attended church since they left their Vietnamese Church

Number of Participants	Age of Participants	Years attending Vietnamese Churches	Denomination
1	22	9	Non attending church
2	22	2	Non attending church
3	23	8	Non attending church
4	25	4	Non attending church
5	26	3	Non attending church
6	26	8	Non attending church
7	22	4	Non attending church
8	21	6	Non attending church
9	21	8	Non attending church
10	20	9	Non attending church
11	25	2	Non attending church
12	26	5	Non attending church
13	26	3	Non attending church
14	27	7	Non attending church
15	29	6	Non attending church
16	23	4	Non attending church
17	25	9	Non attending church
18	25	4	Non attending church
19	25	9	Non attending church
20	25	3	Non attending church
21	25	8	Non attending church
22	26	2	Non attending church

23	26	7	Non attending church
24	25	3	Non attending church
25	24	4	Non attending church
26	24	9	Non attending church
27	20	2	Non attending church
28	20	7	Non attending church
29	19	3	Non attending church
30	19	8	Non attending church
31	20	6	Non attending church
32	20	4	Non attending church
33	21	8	Non attending church
34	21	3	Non attending church
35	21	4	Non attending church
36	25	6	Non attending church
37	25	7	Non attending church
38	24	3	Non attending church
39	26	8	Non attending church
40	24	5	Non attending church
41	23	4	Non attending church
42	21	3	Non attending church
43	20	7	Non attending church
44	21	9	Non attending church
45	22	4	Non attending church
46	20	3	Non attending church
47	23	8	Non attending church
48	20	6	Non attending church
49	22	4	Non attending church
50	26	7	Non attending church
Total Participants	Average Age	Average Years	
	23.14	5.5	

WORKS CITED

Asian American Cultural Awareness. http://www.cedu.niu. edu/~shumow/itt/Asian_American_Cultural_Awareness.pdf. (Accessed Nov. 4th, 2014).

Barna, George. *Leaders on Leadership*. Ventura: Regal, 1997.

Barna, George. *Turnaround Churches: How to Overcome Barriers to Growth and Bring New Life to an Established Church*. Ventura, California: Regal Books, 1993.

Beckwith, Ivy. *Postmodern Children's Ministry: Ministry to Children in the 21st Century*. Grand Rapids, Michigan: Zondervan, 2004.

Bolsinger, Tod E. *It Takes a Church to Raise a Christian: How the Community of God Transforms Lives*. Grand Rapids, Michigan: Brazos Press, 2004.

Cha, Peter. Steve Kang and Helen Lee, eds. *Growing Healthy Asian American Churches: Ministry Insights from Groundbreaking Congregations*. Downers Grove, IL: InterVarsity Press, 2006.

Chacko, Soulit. *Treading Identities: Second-Generation Christian Indian Americans Negotiating Race, Ethnicity and Religion in America*. http://ecommons.luc.edu/cgi/viewcontent.cgi?article=2852&context=luc_theses. (Accessed Feb. 26th, 2015).

Chong, Shiao. *Church and Culture*. http://3dchristianity.wordpress. com/2012/02/03/church-and-culture/. (Accessed Nov. 4th, 2014).

Chun, Sejong. Galatians and Korean Immigrants, http://www.vander-bilt.edu/AnS/religious_studies/GBC/sejongchun.doc. (Accessed Feb. 25th, 2015).

D'Andrade, Roy. *A Study of Personal and Cultural Values: American, Japanese, and Vietnamese.* New York, NY: Palgrave Macmillan, 2008.

Dever, Mark. *Nine Marks of a Healthy Church.* Wheaton, Illinois: Good News Publishers, 2004.

Edwardson, Dale H. *Change it up: Transforming Ordinary Churches into Passionate Disciplemaking Comminities.* Maitland, Florida: Xulonpress, 2013.

Ford, Leighton. *Transforming Leadership: Jesus' Way of Creating Vision, Shaping Values and Empowering Change.* Downers Grove, Illinois: InterVarsity Press, 1991.

Fryling, Robert A. *The Leadership Ellipse: Shaping How We Lead by Who We Are*, Foreword by Eugene H. Peterson. Downer Grove, Illinois: IVP Books, 2010.

Heidhues, Mary Somers, *Southeast Asia: A Concise History.* London: Thames & Hudson, 2000.

Hofstede, Geert, Gert Jan Hofstede, and Michael Minkov. *Cultures and Organizations: Intercultural Cooperation and Its Importance for Survival.* New York: McGraw Hill, 2010.

Huyser-Honig, Joan. *Nine Tips for Designing Intergenerational Worship.* http://worship.calvin.edu/resources/resource-library/nine-tips-for-designing-intergenerational-worship/ (Accessed Feb. 25th, 2015).

Johnson, Channing R. *Where Have All the Young People Gone: Exploring Generational Change and How young People Can be Reached.* Glendale, Arizona: USA, 2012.

Kang, K. Connie. Asian American churches face leadership gap," n.p. *LA Times*, March 03rd, 2007. http://articles.latimes.com/2007/mar/03/local/me-beliefs3 (Accessed January 30th, 2015).

Kim, Elaine H. Home is Where the Han is: A Korean American Perspective on the Los Angeles upheavals. *Social Justice*, 20, (1969).

Kim, Sharon. *A Faith of Our Own: Second-Generation Spirituality in Korean American Churches*. Piscataway, NJ: Rutgers University Press, 2010.

Lee, Helen. "Silent Exodus – Can the East Asian Church in America Reverse the Flight of its Next Generation." *Christianity Today*.

Liu, Yang. *East Meets West: An Infographic Portrait*. http://bsix12.com/east-meets-west/ (Accessed April 9, 2014).

Maxwell, John. *Developing the Leader Within You*. Nashville: Thomas Nelson, 1993.

McGoldrick, Monica, Randy Gerson, and Sueli Petry, *Genograms: Assessment and Intervention*. 3rd ed. New York, NY: W.W. Norton Company, 2007.

Means, James E. *Leadership in Christian Ministry*, Foreword by Kenneth O. Gangel. Grand Rapids, Michigan, Baker Book House, 1989.

Min, Gap Pyong. *Changes and Conflicts: Korean Immigrant Families in New York*. Boston, MA: Allyn and Bacon, 1997.

Min, Pyong Gap and Dae Young Kim, Intergenerational Transmission of Religion and Culture: Korean Protestants in the U.S. *Sociology of Religion, A Quarterly Review*, Vol. 66, Issue 3, pp. 263-282. http://socrel.oxfordjournals.org/content/66/3/263.abstract. (Accessed Feb. 25th, 2015).

Min, Pyong Gap. ed. *Asian American: Contemporary Trends and Issues*. Thousand Oaks, California: Pine Forge Press, 2006.

Mydans, Seth. *Old Soldiers: The Last Refugees Free to Leave Vietnam*, Sept. 14, 1992, *The New York Times*. http://www.nytimes.com/1992/09/14/us/old-soldiers-the-last-refugees-free-to-leave-vietnam.html?src=pm&pagewanted=2&pagewanted=all (Accessed Dec. 16th, 2014).

Nguyen, Ba Quang, *Hội Thánh Ta: Hội Thánh Tin Lành Việt Nam – Giáo Hạt Việt Nam Hoa Kỳ*. Fullerton, California: 2000.

Nguyen, Van Huyen, *The Ancient Civilization of Vietnam*. Hanoi: The Gioi Publishers, 1995.

Nieuwhof, Carey. *Nine Surefire Ways to Make Your Church Completely Ineffective*. Retrieved from http://www.churchleaders.com/pastors/pastor-articles/246803-9-surefire-ways-make-church-completely-ineffective.html. (Accessed on February 9, 2015).

Nixon, David F. *Leading the Comeback Church: Help Your Church Rebound from Decline*. Kansas City, Missouri: Beacon Hill Press of Kansas City, 2004.

Ong, Peter. *Exist Wounds: The Flight of Asian American Faith*. https://peterong.wordpress.com/2006/10/20/exit-wounds-the-flight-of-asian-american-faith-published/ (Accessed Feb. 25th, 2015).

Or, Eunice. *Understanding and Mentorship to Support Second Generation Church Leaders*, http://l2foundation.org/2007/supporting-second-generation-church-leaders. (Accessed February 25th, 2015).

Pang, Valerie Ooka and Li-Rong Lilly Cheng. eds. *Struggling to Be Heard: The Unmet Needs of Asian Pacific American Children*. Albany: State University of New York, 1998.

Park, Jerry Z. and Joshua Tom, *Keeping (and Losing) Faith, the Asian American Way*. http://aapivoices.com/keeping-losing-faith/ (Accessed Feb. 25th, 2015).

Park, Jerry Z. Ethnic Insularity among 1.5 and second-generation Korean-American Christians. *Development and Society*. Vol, 42. No. 1 (June 2013).

Pew Research Center, *Asian Americans: A Mosaic of Faiths.* http://www.pewforum.org/2012/07/19/asian-americans-a-mosaic-of-faiths-overview/ (Accessed January 30, 2015).

Quid of betel consists of a piece of areca-nut and a betel leaf with no lime spread on it, and in some cases, included with a piece of tobacco. Traditionally, Vietnamese people invite their guests to chew betel before starting a conversation. This explains thoroughly the saying known to everyone: "A quid of betel and areca-nut starts the ball rolling." http://www.vietdicts.com/p/16264/trau. (Accessed January 24th, 2014).

Raichur, Ashish. "The Second Generation: Spiritual and Cultural Conflicts" *Agape Partners International.* Cited on 5th November 2014. Online: http://agapepartners.org/articles/34/1/The-Second-GenerationSpiritual-and-Cultural-Conflicts/Page1.html.

Reiland, Dan. *Amplified Leadership: Five Practices to Establish Influence, Build People, and Impact Others for a Lifetime,* Foreword by John C. Maxwell. Lake Mary, Florida: Charisma House Book Group, 2011.

Rupp, George. "1975: The Largest Refugee Resettlement Effort in American History [IRC at 75]." *International Rescue Committee* (June 27th, 2008). Cited 9 April 2014. Online: http://www.rescue.org/blog/1975-largest-refugee-resettlement-effort-american-history-irc-75.

Rutledge, Paul. *The Role of Religion in Ethnic Self-Identity: A Vietnamese Community.* Lanham, New York: University Press of America, 1985.

Saccone, Steve and Cheri Saccone, *Developing Your Next Generation of Church Leaders,* Forword by Mark Batterson. Downers Grove, IL: InterVarsity Press, 2012.

Sander, Oswald J. *Spiritual Leadership: Principles of Experience for Every Believer.* Chicago: Moody Press, 1994.

Sanders, Martin. *The Power of Mentoring: Shaping People Who Will Shape the World* (Camp Hill, Pennsylvania: Christian Publications, Inc. 2004.

Sejong Chun. *Galatians and Korean Immigrants*. http://www.vanderbilt.edu/AnS/religious_studies/GBC/sejongchun.doc. (Accessed February 15th, 2015).

Shellnutt, Kate. *33 Under 33: Meet the Christian leaders shaping the next generation of our faith*. http://www.christianitytoday.com/ct/2014/july-august/33-under-33.html. (Accessed Feb. 25th, 2015).

Sider, Ronald J., Philip N. Olson, and Heidi Rolland Unruh, *Churches that Make a Difference: Reaching Your Community with Good News and Good Works*. Grand Rapids, Michigan: Baker Books, 2002.

Smietana, Bob. *Are Millennials Really Leaving the Church? Yes-but mostly White millennials*. http://www.faithstreet.com/onfaith/2014/05/16/are-millennials-really-leaving-church-yes-but-mostly-white-millennials/32103. (Accessed Feb. 25th, 2015).

Smith, Donald P. *The Mainstream Protestant "Decline": The Presbyterian Pattern*. Eds. Milton J. Coalter, John M. Mulder, and Louis B. Weeks. Louisville, Kentucky: Wesminster/John Knox Press, 1990.

Spector, Ronald H. *Vietnam War*: Encyclopaedia Britannica. http://www.britannica.com/EBchecked/topic/628478/Vietnam-War/234639/The-fall-of-South-Vietnam. (Accessed April 09th, 2014).

Standish, N. Graham. *Humble Leadership: Being Radically Open to God's Guidance and Grace*, Foreword by Diana Butler Bass. Herndon, Virginia: The Alban Institute, 2007.

Stowell, Joseph M. *Shepherding the Church: Effective Spiritual Leadership in a Changing Culture*. Chicago: Moody Press, 1997.

The Online Encyclopedia of Vietnamese Boat People. http://en.wikipedia.org/wiki/Vietnamese_boat_people. (Accessed April 9, 2014).

Ting, Yi-Chya. *Seeking a New Spiritual Home: The Study of Chinese Christian Churches and Communities in the United States.* http://search.proquest.com/docview/304941660. (Accessed Feb. 25th, 2015).

United States Census Bureau. *The Vietnamese Population in the United States: 2010* http://www.bpsos.org/mainsite/images/ DelawareValley/community_profile/us.census.2010.the%20vietnamese%20population_july%202.2011.pdf. (Accessed January 30th, 2015).

Vietnamese Church Annual Report. National Office of the Christian and Missionary Alliance. Received with permission for this dissertation on March 18th, 2015.

Vo, Nghia Minh. *The Vietnamese Boat People, 1954 and 1975— 1992.* Jefferson, North Carolina: McFarland & Company, Inc., Publishers, 2006.

Woods, Shelton L., *Vietnam: A Global Studies Handbook.* California: ABC CLIO, Inc., 2002.

Woods, Shelton. *Vietnam: An Illustrated History.* New York: Hippocrene Books, 2002.

Wuthnow, Robert. *After the Baby Bommers: How Twenty-and Thirty-Somethings Are Shaping the Future of American Religion.* Princeton, NJ: Princeton University Press, 2007.

Yaconelli, Mike. *The Core Relalities of Youth Monistry: Nine Biblical Principles that Mark Healthy Youth Ministry.* Grand Rapids, Michigan: Zondervan, 2003.

Yee, Russell. *Worship on the Way: Exploring Asian North American Christian Experience.* Valley Forge, PA: Judson Press, 2012.

Zimmerman, Kim Ann "What is Culture? Definition of Culture." *Live Science Contributor.* Cited 31 March 2015. Online: http://www. livescience.com/21478-what-is-culture-definition-of-culture.html.

Lightning Source UK Ltd.
Milton Keynes UK
UKHW020056300620
365757UK00016B/4008